William Morris's *Socialist Diary*

William Morris 1887 (Courtesy of the National Portrait Gallery)

William Morris's *Socialist Diary*
Edited and annotated by Florence S. Boos

Five Leaves Publications

William Morris's *Socialist Diary*
Second Edition
Edited and annotated by Florence Boos

Published in 2018 by Five Leaves Publications
14a Long Row, Nottingham NG1 2DH
www.fiveleaves.co.uk
www.fiveleavesbookshop. co.uk

ISBN: 978-1-910170-49-6

Cover images:
Socialist League, 1888, courtesy of the Victoria & Albert Museum
William Morris, 1887, courtesy of the National Portrait Gallery

Printed in Great Britain

Contents

List of Illustrations

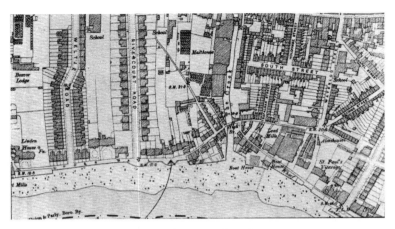

Map of Hammersmith in 1896 (London survey map,
Hammersmith. The Morris house is marked by an arrow.)

Hammersmith Socialist League, photograph c. 1888
People in the photograph mentioned in the *Diary* include Morris,
Emery Walker, James Tochatti, Charles Mordhurst and Henry Tarleton.
(Courtesy of the Victoria and Albert Museum)

Introduction to the First Edition

Morris's achievements routinely exhaust the enumerative abilities of his biographers. When in 1883 William Morris joined the Social Democratic Federation, he had already been a writer of narrative poems and prose romances; pioneer in the decorative arts; translator of Icelandic sagas; designer of stained-glass windows, wallpapers, and tapestries; illuminator of manuscripts; vigorous man of business; founder of the Society for the Protection of Ancient Buildings (SPAB); and loyal personal friend and relation to an impressive range of people.

More relevant to the *Diary* is Morris's identity as the most prominent Victorian artist to embrace the new socialist movement of the 1880s, a choice which was deprecated or condemned by most friends and associates, and some members of his family. From 1883 to 1890, he continued to maintain Morris and Co., and completed several historical prose romances as well as translations, but devoted most of this period to the socialist movement. Several times each week he spoke and attended meetings. He also made strenuous propaganda tours in the North of England and Scotland; kept up a heavy political correspondence with fellow socialists; wrote socialist songs, a long poem on the Paris Commune, a socialist play, and historical and utopian romances; defended socialist and related causes in innumerable letters to newspapers; edited and wrote weekly for the socialist newspaper *Commonweal* after 1885; and led from 1885 to 1890 one of England's two major socialist organisations, the Socialist League.

Some of the literary work of this period was among the best he ever wrote. His translations declined in number but not quality, and several of his socialist poems are excellent. *A Dream of John Ball* and *News from Nowhere* are the most well-known and admired of his prose works, and his short, pithy political commentaries in *Commonweal* helped to make it the most vigorous and sophisticated leftist publication of its decade.[1] In addition, he wrote many socialist essays from 1883–94, several of

---

[1]   For a comparative study of socialist periodicals of the period, see James G. Coolsen, 'The Evolution of Major English Socialist Periodicals, 1883-1889,' Diss., American University, 1973. A comprehensive discussion of the radical press of the period is found in Elizabeth Miller, *Slow Print: Literary Radicalism and Late Victorian Print Culture*, Stanford University Press, 2013.

which he himself never published in full or in chronological order.[2] Direct and rhythmic in cadence, they reflect the intense simplicity which Morris considered appropriate for dignified popular art.

During this period, Morris's personal example and dedication inspired and encouraged members of every faction of the left, and his decisions had a strong effect on the origins of British socialism. But the influence of his political prescriptions and theoretic emphases waned quickly after his death in 1896, and both his actions and his views have since been reassessed many times. Morris was an impressive eclectic, and representatives of all parties have argued that he anticipated or approved their endeavours — Fabians, anarcho-communists, parliamentarians, trade unionists, art societies, all shades of gradualists and revolutionaries, ethical socialists, members of the Independent Labour Party (ILP); even, grotesquely, anti-communists. Inevitably, some of these reinterpretations have led to dubious projection and misappropriation. British socialism of the 1880s was so riven by faction and isolated from mainstream political discourse that both activists and later historians have tried many times to recast the sequence of events — could and should Morris have behaved differently, could he have united an effective socialist workers' movement, were his stances politically consistent, or valid, or constructive? Morris's decisions were intelligent and tolerant, but sometimes idiosyncratic. Often they seem to reflect Morris's personal heroism, and a tendency in his view of socialism to polarise the very concrete and the very distant — immediate propaganda, and the ideal future society. In his other endeavours this 'idealism' had united in pragmatic form a strong individual creative drive and a deep perception of kinship with others; here it could seem more a heroic exemplar than a pattern for imitation.

Yet is this a legitimate reproach? In the British socialist movement of the '80s, continental exiles already strained against advocates for a nascent electoral politics and trade-unionism; and this divergence was

---

[2]   See Eugene LeMire, *Unpublished Lectures of William Morris*, 1969; Paul Meier, 'An Unpublished Lecture of William Morris: How Shall We Live Then?' *International Review of Social History* 16, part 2 (1970); and Florence Boos, *Our Country Right or Wrong, by William Morris*, London: William Morris Society, 2008; 'William Morris's "Equality": A Critical Edition,' *Journal of Pre-Raphaelite Studies* 20 n. s. (Spring 2011); 'William Morris's 'Commercial War': A Critical Edition,' *JPRS*, no. 19 (winter 2010); and 'Two Unpublished Morris Essays: Morris's "Socialism" and "What We Have to Look For,"' *Journal of William Morris Studies* 18.4 (Winter 2010).

probably inherent. The fragmentation of the 'anarchist', 'reformist', and 'collectivist' factions of the British socialist movement may have been unpreventable, and it is perhaps to Morris's credit that he successfully harmonised these still-creative tensions as long as he did, and offered moderate admonitions and qualified support in the final years of his life to several of the divergent parties.

Morris's *Socialist Diary* of 1887 is one of the most interesting writings from this period of his work. It is one of only two extended diaries of his activities which he kept in his life, each of which represents an effort to record and analyse experiences of a new phase of his work and thought. His 1871 and 1873 *Journals of Travels to Iceland* embody a commitment to Icelandic literature which inspired many of his efforts during the next two decades. The much briefer *Socialist Diary* was kept during a period of intense activity from January to April 1887, and until recently had never been published in its entirety. Its brevity and bluntness render it a more accessible introduction to his political activities and beliefs than the editorial notes of *Commonweal*, his more expansive essays, or his massive socialist correspondence to friends and comrades during this period. Morris's tactical analyses give a shrewd but admirably disinterested view of many of the political groups of his time: Gladstonian liberalism and the Liberal Unionists, Bradlaughian radicalism, Fabianism, Hyndman's Social Democratic Federation, several varieties of anarchism, and the anti-parliamentarian and parliamentarian wings of the Socialist League. The *Diary* also records grim economic conditions, hostility of the newspapers and police, shifting responses of his audiences, and practical obstacles to his efforts at propaganda. Finally, it documents some of the movement's many achievements — its genuine intellectual variety and cooperation under stress, and a sense of excitement and anticipation, which deepened as well as intensified its doctrinal and tactical disputes.

Like the *Icelandic Journals*, the *Socialist Diary* represents an effort to concretise and analyse the activities of a period of transition. In early 1887 Morris had already been an active socialist for four years, working throughout this period to encourage the mass movement he knew was necessary for the achievement of socialism, and for almost two years he had struggled to unite the non-Hyndman elements of the socialist movement around a common programme in the Socialist League. The *Diary* records his understated but honest assessment of the factors which would frustrate both of these goals and eventually exclude him from

3

active political leadership outside of the local Hammersmith Socialist Society. Written after the completion of the visionary *A Dream of John Ball*, and before the suppression of the Trafalgar Square Demonstration of November 1887, the *Diary* provides a good indication of Morris's reactions at the midpoint of his period of most vigorous activity. It has been claimed that the Trafalgar Square police attack darkened his view of the immediate possibilities for socialism. It certainly demonstrated the helplessness of untrained, unarmed demonstrators when faced with military attack, but the *Diary* clearly indicates that Morris had never been sanguine about the immediate effectiveness of socialist agitation.

At an early stage Morris seems to have thought of publishing his diary; he wrote to his daughter Jenny that he had begun an account of his socialist activities which might be useful later on, 'a sort of Jonah's eye view of the whale, you know,' and early in the *Diary* he pauses several times to explain items that might not have needed clarification in a private document — at one point, for example, he notes 'for the benefit of well-to-do West-Enders' the familiar pattern of police brutality toward the poor.

Why then did Morris put it aside after only three months? The obvious answer is overwork. The weekly *Commonweal* of this period was in itself a massive labour, demanding detailed narrations of meetings and political events which he would also have described in the *Diary*. When parallel accounts of similar events in the *Diary*, *Commonweal*, and letters to his daughters and other socialists became impossible, Morris probably decided that letters and journalism were commitments he could not suspend. Most immediately, the Scottish campaign distracted him from his usual schedule, and material which might otherwise have seemed more suitable for a semi-private journal was placed directly into the articles on his travels. The *Diary* as it stands may have accomplished its essential purpose of enabling Morris to analyse patterns of socialist agitation and formulate his own views more clearly, as expressed in the essays which he wrote during the year, including 'Monopoly', 'Feudal England', 'The Policy of Abstention', 'The Society of the Future', and 'The Present Outlook in Politics'. Also the tension between parliamentarians and anti-parliamentarians which preceded the 1887 Conference may have seemed too factionalised for a semi-public document, and during the next months he diverted his time to writing urgent letters to potential allies, and to private and public reformulations of his arguments against palliation, compromise, and parliamentarianism.

The *Diary* has suffered an uneven fate at the hands of biographers, beginning with J. W. Mackail, who published *The Life of William Morris*, 1899, and a mildly sympathetic account of Morris's socialism in a pamphlet, *William Morris*, 1901. In his biography Mackail published long excerpts from the *Diary*, but he omitted passages describing Morris's more productive campaigns in the North, and highlighted accounts of the movement's internal debates and failures. A classical scholar who was by temperament more retiring than Morris, Mackail summarised the *Diary*'s contents in dour reduction:

> The extracts which follow show what immense labour he continued to spend in the service of the League, and how clearly nevertheless he saw the weakness of their machinery and the futility of the greater part of their efforts, and of his own. (vol. II p. 169)

By contrast May Morris greatly respected her father's socialist writings but, as Eugene LeMire has carefully documented in his introduction to *The Unpublished Lectures of William Morris* (1969), was pressured by both executors and publishers to reprint as little as possible of the lesser-known works, especially the socialist writings. Perhaps in compensation, she tended to smuggle favourite portions of these writings, in confusing sequence, into her introductions to the *Collected Works*. In two of the four volumes in which she describes Morris's socialist activity in greatest detail — numbers 20 and 23 — she prints additional passages, and two decades later she published further excerpts in *William Morris Artist Writer Socialist*. Although some sense of the *Diary*'s contents can be obtained from these fragments, their publication did little to further appreciation of its literary and political unity. E.P. Thompson's *William Morris: Romantic to Revolutionary* (1955; 2nd ed. 1977) cites the *Socialist Diary* in considerable detail, and responds sympathetically to the intensity and vigour of Morris's speaking trips to Scotland, but Thompson's own electoral Marxism may cause him to de-emphasise Morris's anti-parliamentarian associations during this period and to deprecate his commitment to labour issues. Of Morris's energetic propaganda among the striking miners, Thompson writes:

> Morris appears to have failed to realize either the importance of the possibilities opened up by this foothold in the coalfields or the gravity of the defeat. (2nd ed. p. 438)

In April Morris proposed to the Council a Hyde Park meeting in support of the miners' strike and the socialists' northern campaign. To him, the failed strike seemed only one of a number of signs (not least among them the general apathy of London audiences) of the desperate situation of the proletariat.

Throughout the *Diary* Morris reflects on obstacles to the progress of socialism. In several glances backward, he despairs once again of parliamentary Liberalism, and his distaste for the Radical Clubs never wavers. His response to the tactics of the Socialist League's chief rival, H.M. Hyndman's Social Democratic Federation (SDF), is more complex. With other secessionists from the SDF, he had been repelled by Hyndman's 'vanguardism', his insistence on personal and secretive control of London and provincial branches, and his evenhanded condescension towards the two groups that inevitably comprised most members of the party, foreign *emigrés* and members of the working class. Upon leaving the SDF Morris wrote:

> [Hyndman's] aim has been to make the movement seem big, to frighten the powers that be with a turnip bogie which perhaps he almost believes in himself: hence all that insane talk of immediate forcible revolution, when we know that the workers in England are not even touched by the movement; hence the founding of branches which melt away into mere names, the neglect of organization for fruitless agitation; and worst of all, hence discreditable intrigue and sowing of suspicion among those who are working for the party. (BL Add. MS, 45, 345, letter to Joynes, Christmas Day 1884; Kelvin 2:354)

> 1. ... We have formed another body, the Socialist League... it expects singleheartedness from its members and fraternal co-operation, and... will not suffer any absolutism amongst it. (letter to Robert Thompson, 1 January 1885, Henderson, *Letters*, p. 229; Kelvin 2:369)

Morris's objections to the antecedents of 'democratic centralism' were deeply rooted in conviction and temperament, and associated in his own mind with his anti-parliamentarianism and preference for local organisation loosely interwoven by international ties.

Quite specifically, he attacked Hyndman's threats against the government, attempts to conceal the movement's limited following, and

Socialist League membership card
(Courtesy of Special Collections, University of Maryland)

his nationalism, as, among other things, a failure of socialist imagination as well as integrity:

> Hence attacks on foreigners as foreigners or at least sneers at them: coquetting also with jingoism in various forms, all of which mean waiting about to see what can be made of the political situation, if perhaps at the best one may attain to a sort of Bismarckian State Socialism, or as near it as we can get in England. I cannot stand all this, it is not what I mean by Socialism either in aim or in means: I want a real revolution, a real change in Society: Society a great organic mass of well-regulated forces used for the bringing about a happy life for all... the revolution cannot be a mechanical one, though the last act of it may be civil war, or it will end in reaction after all. (to Robert Thompson, 1 January 1885, Henderson, *Letters*, p. 228; Kelvin 2:368)

Morris is also wary of street demonstrations of the unemployed; unless they anticipate the rising of an entire class, they manipulate the misery of their participants, and provoke needless arrests.

> Well, it is a mistake to try to organise riot... yet... any opposition to law and order in the streets is of use to us, if the price of it is not too high... (10 February 1886, in Arnot, p. 79; Kelvin 2: 520)

> Take this for my word about this kind of thing: if a riot is quite spontaneous it does frighten the bourgeois even if it's but isolated; but planned riots or shows of force are not good unless in a time of action, when they are backed by the opinion of the people and are in point of fact indications of the rising tide. (16 February, *Diary*).

He would later argue in similar terms about 'propaganda of the deed' and sporadic appeals to popular violence, that mindless taunts to the authorities would be suicidal, if they failed to reflect a rising tide of consistent feeling.

Traditionally, the most difficult to understand of Morris's tactical convictions is his deep opposition to electoral politics. Even in the early days of the Socialist League (SL), his aggressive opposition to socialist parliamentary campaigns was shared by few, especially outside of London. Almost all of the Marxists associated with the Socialist League — Eleanor Marx, Edward Aveling, Engels, A.K. Donald, and E.B. Bax

— were parliamentarists from the beginning, and his allies from the provinces — Bruce Glasier, John Glasse, Tom Maguire — all abandoned their anti-electoralism in later years. More to the point, the resulting dispute eventually incapacitated the SL, and led to its division in 1888. Efforts by the Socialist Union, J.L. Mahon and the North of England Federation, the Labour Emancipation League, H.H. Champion, the Labour Union, the SDF, and others to elect socialists were unsuccessful before the London County Council elections of 1891, but not as overwhelmingly so as the SDF's first campaigns of 1885 (in which its two London candidates, John Williams and John Fielding, had polled a total of fifty-nine votes).

Yet Morris's proposed alternatives — education of the entire working class to socialism, followed by an uprising of the workers — receded constantly from view. Morris also had similar reservations about other provisional or 'palliative' measures — co-operative stores, or campaigns for free speech in the parks — which he nevertheless supported as legitimate forms of training in propaganda and organisation. By contrast Morris's *Diary* and political letters of the period indicate that his single greatest concern may have been to prevent the League Council of 1887 from taking a parliamentary position.

Several of Morris's associates and later commentators — Fabians, members of the ILP, Marxists — have argued that Morris later changed his mind. For example, Hyndman wrote that in a speech in 1895, Morris supported his parliamentary campaign and retracted his former opposition. In *William Morris and the Early Days of the Socialist Movement*, Bruce Glasier, by then a supporter of the ILP, writes that Morris expressed encouragement and approval in 1895 of gains by the Labour Party. (p. 134) Several later editors and historians have followed suit (e.g, A.L. Morton, ed., *Political Writings of William Morris*, 1973, p. 241). There is no such evidence of reconciliation with the Fabians. Robin Page Arnot records that when he asked Sidney Webb what Morris had said to him after an 1895 Hammersmith SL lecture, Webb reported Morris's parting remark: 'The world is going your way at the present, Webb, but it is not the right way in the end.' (Arnot, p. 108) In any case, the issue of electoral politics was the central one in Morris's relation to the League. It is important therefore to define carefully his position in 1887, ask why he defended it so heatedly, even at the cost of further active political influence, and inquire whether his later statements do represent a genuine change in view.

The most restrained version of Morris's 1887 position was that he saw several alternate forms of socialist endeavour — parliamentarianism among them — but felt that the SDF was a parliamentary party, and so the SL should choose an alternate form of effort. This conception of a confederated movement with several harmonious and alternate strategies for propaganda is an attractive one, and Morris did use such grounds to urge J.L. Mahon and other SL parliamentarians to retun to the SDF. A similar view appears in letters to Glasse:

> ... to have two organisations holding the same tenets and following the same policy seems to me absurd. (19 May 1887, Arnot, p. 82; Kelvin 2:657)

> I appeal to those who doubt the usefulness of such a body of principle at all events to stand aside and not to break it up but join other bodies now existing for whom I for my part feel complete tolerance, so long as they are not brought inside ours. (23 May 1887, Arnot, p. 83; Kelvin 2:658)

Even here a crucial qualification enters in the determination that the SL and parliamentarians must be completely disjoint: the SL itself can contain no parliamentary wing. In all his evaluations, Morris clearly considers his educationalist-revolutionarism the superior position. Parliamentarianism inevitably requires vitiating compromise, and a vigorous association of extra-parliamentary socialists must reassert the movement's original aims. This mixture of tolerance and distaste appears in his remarks to John Glasse on 23 May 1887, a month after the *Diary* ends, and shortly before the Conference on 30 May.

> I believe that the Socialists will certainly send members to Parliament when they are strong enough to do so: in itself I see no harm in that, so long as it is understood that they go there as rebels, not as members of the governing body, prepared by passing palliative measures to keep 'Society' alive. But I fear that many of them will be drawn into that error by the corrupting influence of a body professedly hostile to Socialism: and therefore I dread the parliamentary period (clearly a long way ahead at present) of the progress of the party; and I think it will be necessary always to keep alive a body of Socialists of principle who will refuse responsibility for the actions of the parliamentary portion of the party... I repeat, the non-parliamentary feeling will assuredly not be repressed entirely. (Arnot, pp. 82-83; Kelvin 2:658)

More harshly, his letters and essays of the period charge that palliative measures create active harm, by distracting people from true awareness of their degradation and servitude. For example, on 30 March 1887, he wrote to Joseph Lane:

> Meanwhile I believe all palliative measures like the 8 hours bill to be delusive, and so, damaging to the cause if *put forward by socialists as a part of socialism*: though of course they will be put forward and carried at some time by some party, and we shall then have to take the good and the bad of them. But we should be clear that *they are not our measures*. I think the duty of the League is educational entirely at present; and that duty is all the more important since the SDF has entirely given up that side of things. (BL Add. MS. 45,345; Kelvin 2:631)

Later in the year he formulated his position more explicitly in 'The Policy of Abstention':

> ... I cannot help thinking that the scheme of parliament would be found in practice to stand in the way of the formation of that widespread organization with its singleness of aim and directness of action which it seems to me is what we want: that the effort towards success in parliament will swallow up all other effort, that such success in short will come to be looked upon as the end... the organization I am thinking of would have a serious point of difference from any that could be formed as a part of a parliamentary plan of action: its aim would be to act directly, whatever was done in it would be done by the people themselves; there would consequently be no possibility of compromise, of the association becoming anything else than it was intended to be; nothing could take its place: before all its members would be put but one alternative to complete success, complete failure, namely. Can as much be said for any plan involving the representatives of the people forming a part of a body whose purpose is the continuous enslavement of the people? (*AWS*, vol. II p. 447)

In a farewell to the SL written three and a half years later, Morris made the point more epigrammatically:

> ... there are a great many who believe it possible to compel their masters by some means or another to behave better to them, and though they are prepared to compel them (by so-called peaceful means, strikes and the like), all but a very small

> minority are not prepared *to do without masters*. ('Where Are
> We Now?' Morton, ed., *Political Writings*, p. 225)

Interwoven with Morris's anti-reformism was his deep ethical contempt for the activity of politicians: so fundamentally a matter of sordid compromise and dishonest temporary alliances did parliamentary activity seem to him. Something of this real hostility surfaces in the contexts in which he describes Hyndman and Donald as intriguers and 'politicians', and in his sharp exchange with the increasingly parliamentary J.L. Mahon, directly before and after the Conference of 1887. If the parliamentarians do take over the League, Morris asserts, the League itself will be destroyed:

> Finally you must not forget that whatever open steps I might take, I personally would have nothing to do with politics properly so called. The whole business is so revolting to a decent quiet body with an opinion of his own, that if that were our road, I should not be able to help dropping off it. (17 May, Arnot, p. 66; Kelvin 2:653)

> If the League does disappear, I shall try to get a dozen men together whom I can trust, and who have definite ideas about socialism and decline anybody who doesn't really hold these views: I will speak and write wherever I can: but I will not give one penny to support any set of people who won't come up to the test. (14 June, Arnot, p. 68; Kelvin 2:667)

Later in the year he concluded a lecture on 'The Present Outlook in Politics' with the hope that in a new society politics as we know them may be completely superseded:

> It is certain that even now while we speak politics of the old kind, the shuffle of Ins and Outs, are waning away, and the new politics that are taking the place of the old mean a struggle against stupidity for the reconstruction of society on a tolerable instead of intolerable basis, so that at last we may be led into the happy days when society shall be what its name means, and politics will be no more. (LeMire, *Unpublished Lectures of William Morris*, p. 216)

And as late as 1895, in a lecture on 'What We Have to Look For', he speaks of the immediate future as filled with

> … failure and disappointment and stupidity and causeless quarrels, and in short all the miseries that go to make up the degrading game of politics. (*AWS*, vol. II p. 358)

The paradox of a political movement founded on contempt for existing politics is perhaps too familiar for further comment. During this period at least, Morris was actively hostile to the argument that an electoral campaign could itself be educational and provide expression for the more theoretical formulations of the League.

One wonders what influence the character of the socialist parliamentarians of 1887 had on Morris's 'theoretical' position. Morris felt active contempt for the motives and actions of Hyndman, Aveling, and Donald; he had no moral objections to Mahon and Champion, but indicates in the letters that he considered them misguided and changeable. He seems to have been only peripherally concerned with Engels's views, and saw Eleanor Marx as essentially an adjunct of Aveling. Bax's abstruse and theoretical manner may have undercut the persuasiveness of his tactical arguments, and Morris seems to have felt little active sympathy with any of the Fabians except Shaw.

By contrast Morris's letters indicate consistent respect for anti-parliamentarians such as Joseph Lane, and perhaps more significantly, for such anti-parliamentarian foreign refugees as Peter Kropotkin (and perhaps to a lesser extent for Victor Dave, Henry Charles, and Sergius Stepniak).

One should perhaps keep in mind that Morris's great model for revolutionary heroism was the Paris Commune. The émigré-Communards' internationalism, revolutionary histories, and obvious sufferings on behalf of the cause elicited Morris's sympathy for heroic defeats and his sense of alliance in a continuing struggle. Hyndman's association of jingoism and parliamentarianism seemed to suggest an opposite stance. Finally, elements of Morris's fears became reality: internationalism *was* submerged, mainstream socialism *did* become narrowly British, reformist ministers *did* break strikes and suppress all anarchist or syndicalist impulses.

All the same: if 'politics' were inevitably contaminated, what political means could the League use to effect the total reversal of economic relationships? For Morris the solution to this enigma lay in an alternate vision of worker organisation: he wanted a separate government by workers, as it were a Labour Parliament, which would eventually assert its alternate legitimacy to rule.

> … as the approaching break-down of the monopolist system comes closer conviction will be forced on the minds of more and more people, till at last the mere necessities of life will force the main part of the workers to join them…

> The revolutionary body will find its duties divided into two parts, the maintenance of its people while things are advancing to the final struggle, and resistance to the constitutional authority, including the evasion or disregard of the arbitrary laws of the latter. Its chief weapons during this period will be co-operation and boycotting... ('The Policy of Abstention', *AWS*, vol. II p. 448)

Marxist views of recent revolutions, and their greater likelihood of occurrence in nations where capitalism had evolved to its most intense and self-defeating level of organisation, may have contributed to Morris's intransigence. So also may the analogy of Home Rule. If the revolutionary Irish could advocate election of their own representatives outside of Parliament, why not the proletariat? Recall also the parliament of early 1887: Conservative-dominated, with not a single working-class member independent of the Liberals, and only one maverick quasi-socialist aristocrat, R.B. Cunninghame-Graham, soon to be ostracised for his part in the Trafalgar Square Demonstration of November 1887. In this light, Morris's impatience with 'permeation' may seem more understandable. Freed from a hereditary upper house and reactionary monarch, a truly independent Labour Parliament could make clear pronouncements and set its own suffrage requirements (presumably universal adult suffrage). Its very existence would threaten the established government and publicise the socialist cause among the workers.

Ironically, Morris may well have been confirmed in his opposition to electoral politics by sincere, rather than verbal, commitment to revolutionary determinism and the monolithic outlines of Marx's model for the fall of capitalism. If as Marx claimed, capitalism was a self-defeating system of oppression which would exhaust itself in overproduction for increasingly scarce markets; and if, as Marx and Morris both believed, labour not only ought to be but in fact was the only source of value and wealth; then accommodation with an exploitive system would only increase the wealth of capitalists, and decrease the power of labour:

> ... at present when the rights of capital are admitted and all that is claimed is a proportional share in the profits, it means a kind of relief to the employers, an additional poor-rate levied from the workers... (*AWS*, vol.II p. 443)

Or degenerate into hypocrisy:

> Any other programme is misleading and dishonest; it has two faces to it, one of which says to the working-man, 'This is Socialism or the beginning of it' (which it is not), and the other says to the capitalist, 'This is sham Socialism; if you can get the workers, or part of them, to accept this, it will create a new lower middle class, a buffer, to push in between Privilege and Socialism, and save you, if only for a while.' (*CW*, vol.XXIII p. 253, 'Monopoly')

To talk of redistributing wealth, but avoid the issue of self-determination, was a mere fantasy:

> Well the masters can and do reply: My friends... we know your interest better than you do yourselves, and shall resist your feeble attempts to reduce our salaries; and since we organize your labour and the market of the world which it supplies, we shall manage your wages amongst other matters. (*AWS*, vol. II p. 443)

Morris may have been wrong. But these quotations should effectively refute the view that his position was literary-utopian or 'naive'.

Which is not to say that other motives did not reinforce his intransigence. All his life — in his poetry, narrative fantasies, friendships, and his work for the Firm — Morris sought to promote a kind of idealised comradeship which strained against the resort to compromise for (alleged) immediate tactical gains. He was capable of sustained hard work of almost incredible intensity; but gradualism and bargain-cutting were as remote from his natural mode of action as from his imaginative efforts. In Morris's early poetry, a protagonist often holds out nobly against insuperable odds in the name of fellowship, justice, and love; in the quest-allegories of his maturity, such as the *Earthly Paradise* tales, the protagonist breaks the frame of each partially completed journey and begins anew. Had Morris been content to live less the spirit of his searching, poetic protagonists, he would never have 'betrayed his class interests' and embraced revolutionary socialism in the first place. His refusal or inability to coerce others or reduce a unified vision to its more 'practical' components expressed the same anger and compassion as did his political engagement. A 'political' temperament, which might have made Morris a good parliamentarian, Fabian, or trade-unionist at fifty-three, might also have frozen him in any number of earlier, more 'reasonable' bourgeois roles; for example: (i) as a Christian socialist at twenty (his mother had wanted him to become a bishop, and as a young man he was fond of ecclesiastical lore); or (ii) as a restorationist architect at twenty-five (he apprenticed in the firm of G.B. Street, the most enlightened practitioner of exactly the sort of restoration Morris later bitterly opposed); or (iii) as a Gladstonian Liberal MP at forty (his friends' expectation).

The restless irritation with which he rejected all these plausibly trimmed expressions of middle-class liberalism may have reflected an acutely heightened awareness of the nature and ease of co-optation. Morris was one of the few who debated the issue of electoralism for whom a 'successful' political career as a suitably trimmed 'maverick' would in fact have been readily available. He was always conscious of the fact that his environment clearly encouraged what he considered defections from duty, and discouraged self-sacrifice. He wrote to Georgiana Burne-Jones:

> Meantime what a little ruffles me is this, that if I do a little fail in my duty some of my friends will praise me for failing instead of blaming me. (31 October 1885, Henderson, *Letters*, p. 242; Kelvin 2:480)

To someone to whom compromise and partial success were always available, voluntary assumption of defeat came to seem a test of sincerity:

> We must get used to such trifles as defeats, and refuse to be discouraged by them. Indeed I am an old hand at that game, my life having been passed in being defeated; as surely as every man's must be who finds himself forced into a position a little ahead of the average in his aspirations. (letter, 15 August 1887, to Bruce Glasier, *CW*, vol.XX p. xlvii; Kelvin 2:684)

One can also invoke his class background and privilege to support quite different critical arguments about Morris's purism. Did his financial security influence his relative opposition to immediate political gains such as the eight-hour day or increased hourly wages? He himself drew a more complex connection:

> ... in my position of a well-to-do man, not suffering from the disabilities which oppress a working man at every step, I feel

that I might never have been drawn into the practical side of the question if an ideal had not forced me to seek towards it. For politics as politics, i.e. not regarded as a necessary if cumbersome and disgustful means to an end, would never have attracted me, nor when I had become conscious of the wrongs of society as it now is, and the oppression of poor people, could I ever have believed in the possibility of a *partial* setting right of those wrongs. In other words, I could never have been such a fool as to believe in the happy and 'respectable' poor. ('How I Became a Socialist', Morton, *Political Writings*, p. 243)

'Perhaps some of my desires for the new society will seem strange to you,' he told an audience in 1887, but:

One reason which will make some of you think them strange is a sad and shameful one. I have always belonged to the well-to-do classes, and was born into luxury, so that necessarily I ask much more of the future than many of you do; and the first of all my visions, and that which colours all my others, is of a day when that misunderstanding will no longer be possible; when the words poor and rich, though they will still be found in our dictionaries, will have lost their old meaning... (*AWS*, vol II pp. 455-56)

When Joseph Lane left the SL in 1889, he criticised Morris rather sharply, and Morris responded as follows:

As to your estimate of my character, I am not going to dispute that, not even the fool part of it; indeed there is much truth in it — fool and all. You see (and I mean this in all soberness) you must make allowance for a man born and bred in the very heart of capitalism, and remember that however he may rebel against the sham society of today we are all damaged by it. (BL Add. MS. 45,345, 21 May 1889; Kelvin 3:68)

A suggestive analogy can be drawn with Peter Kropotkin: also favoured by birth, he had renounced professional and hereditary favours to espouse the cause of the oppressed; he also distrusted reformism, envisioned the ultimate realignment of society, and believed in patient education toward a mass uprising. Morris, of course, was not an aristocrat, but the self-employed son of a prosperous banker. His analysis of repression was intimately anti-capitalist, but one cannot readily deduce his anti-electoralism from his middle-class origins, at least not without some auxiliary hypotheses: most of the Fabian and parliamentary Marxists from whom he differed — Engels, Hyndman, Aveling, Champion, A.K. Donald, E.B. Bax — were fellow bourgeois, after all. True, they did not spend an early boyhood on a wooded estate. But Morris's response to this environment, however, like Kropotkin's to the beauty and complexity of nature, was his own. Asked by Wilfred Blunt whether a love of beauty was hereditary, he replied:

> 'As for me,' he said, 'I have it naturally, for neither my father nor my mother nor any of my relatives had the least idea of it. I remember as a boy going into Canterbury Cathedral and thinking that the gates of Heaven had been opened to me — also when I first saw an illuminated manuscript. These first pleasures, which I discovered for myself, were stronger than anything else I have had in life. (BL Add. MS. 45,350, f.40)

This sense of isolation both deepened the fierceness and ardour of many of Morris's responses, and aroused an intense desire for a wider fellowship and community.

Whatever its origins, Morris's sense of detachment, fairness, and identification with any fellow workers led to a deep contempt for politics as a combative middle-class game, or even a forum for electoral-socialist 'leadership'. Morris seldom spoke directly of the deepest motives for his acts. A long and carefully reasoned letter written soon after his conversion to socialism to a distant acquaintance, C. E. Maurice (1843-1927) a Christian Socialist, is a rare revelation of the insights which impelled him to socialism:

> … furthermore in looking into matters social and political I have but one rule, that in thinking of the condition of any body of men I should ask myself, 'How could you bear it yourself? What would you feel if you were poor against the system under which you live?' I have always been uneasy when I had to ask myself that question, and of late years I have had to ask it so often, that I have seldom had it out of my mind: and the answer to it has more and more made me ashamed of my own position, and more and more made me feel that if I had not been born rich or well-to-do I should have found my position unendurable, and should have been a mere rebel against what would have seemed to me a system of robbery and injustice. Nothing can argue me out of this feeling… the contrasts of rich

and poor are unendurable and ought not to be endured by either rich or poor. (1 July 1883, Henderson, *Letters*, p. 176; Kelvin 2:202)

Something close to utter alienation emerges from his letters of the period:

> A society which is founded on the system of compelling all well-to-do people to live on making the greatest possible profit out of the labour of others, must be wrong. For it means the perpetuation of the division of society into civilized and uncivilized classes: I am far from being an anarchist, but even anarchy is better than this, which is in fact anarchy and despotism mixed: if there is no hope of conquering this — let us eat and drink, for tomorrow we die. (9 September 1883, to T.C. Horsfall, Henderson, *Letters*, p. 182; Kelvin 2:225)

> Whatever hope or life there is in me is staked on the success of the cause: I believe you object to the word: but I know no other to express what I mean. (1 June 1884, to Georgiana Burne-Jones, Henderson, *Letters*, p. 200; Kelvin 2:286)

Parallel remarks appear in Morris's earliest and latest political lectures. He seems to have felt the greatest desire to reflect on his emotional and intellectual motives at the beginning and end of his efforts. Since adolescence, he had written poetry whose protagonists express despair at the entrapment of sordid human environments. Gradually, and with great effort, he came to conceptualise a social equivalent (source? analogy? correlative?) for this discontent. In the 1884 lecture, 'Misery and the Way Out', Morris breaks into a more drastic declaration than his audience may have expected:

> Is it so indeed? yet here I stand before you, one of the most fortunate of this happy class, so steeped in discontent, that I have no words which will express it: no words, nothing but deeds, wherever they may lead me to, even [if] it be ruin, prison, or a violent death. (*AWS*, vol II p. 156)

Seldom has such 'merely personal' and 'individual' restlessness combined more intelligently with perception of an all-penetrating social wrong. The creator of the Launcelot of 'King Arthur's Tomb' and Bodli of 'The Lovers of Gudrun' had found a more adequate and comprehensive plot, and one that required a different audience.

Morris was always a graceful loser, ready to acknowledge that his opponent may have acted for the better after all. For this reason, I believe, reports of his later acceptance of electoralism have been exaggerated: Hyndman and Glasier may have blurred just such self-deprecating and carefully qualified nuances of his casual speech. As Morris's health made active political work less possible, he became anxious that such contacts as he could make were for the encouragement of socialist unity. His earlier position had been on the order of: palliative efforts may achieve some results, but I wish to devote myself to a more radical effort. The nuanced emphases of his public statements of the 1890s (often made to people who had made different choices) were: though I do not find these methods or goals most urgent or beneficial, the achievement of limited reforms may be useful in preparing us for the (greatly more desirable) next stage of socialism (for which I had chiefly hoped to work).

Even then, tensions remain between his desires to praise, and to give warning that immediate goals must serve long-term ones. On 10 March 1893, Morris delivered a lecture to the Hammersmith Socialist Society on 'Communism', passages from which are sometimes cited as an example of his shift in opinions about tactics as well as ultimate aims. Again Morris freely admits the uncontroversial: that if reforms can encourage the strength of labourers' desire for equality and co-operation, they will achieve real good:

> … if the sum of them should become vast and deep reaching enough to give to the useful or working-classes intelligence enough to conceive of a life of equality and co-operation; courage enough to accept it and to bring the necessary skill to bear on working for it; and power enough to force its acceptance on the stupid and the interested, the war of classes would speedily end in the victory of the useful class, which would then become the new Society of Equality. (*Political Writings*, p. 229)

Notice however the many conjuncts to his hypothesis. After he has acquitted himself of these, and other, heavily qualified, endorsements, he returns to his familiar warning:

> For the Social-democratic measures above mentioned are all of them either makeshift alleviations to help us through the present days of oppression, or means for landing us in the new country of equality. And there is a danger that they will be looked upon as ends in themselves. (*Political Writings*, pp. 233-34)

Morris did not really reverse himself about reformism-as-co-opted-revolution; he suspended the debate. Perhaps he simply decided at the end of his life that reformism was an inevitable evil, and that he would have to plead his case in more conciliatory terms.

May Morris cites similarly reluctant passages from another partially recorded lecture on 'Communism' of the same period, as evidence of her father's changed view:

> I confess I am no great lover of political tactics; the sordid squabble of an election is unpleasant enough for a straightforward man to deal in: yet I cannot fail to see that it is necessary somehow to get hold of the machine which has at its back the executive power of the country, however that may be done... (*AWS*, vol II p. 350; 'Communism — i.e. Property,' ed. F. Boos, *WMS-US Newsletter*, Summer, 2009)

Even in the 1887 letters to Glasse and Glasier, Morris had accepted that parliamentarianism was an inevitable obstruction to be mastered or overcome, '... however that may be done'. What he rejected was the proposition that this was a method sufficiently radical to serve as a programme for socialists. In one of his last published public addresses, made in 1894 to the Ancoats Fellowship of Manchester, he has nothing but praise for Robert Blatchford, the *Clarion*, and other 'sturdy labourers' for socialism, but the goodwill of such a parting gesture does not completely obscure more characteristic admonitions against half-measures:

> Let us... take care that our present struggle leaves behind it no class distinction, but brings about one condition of equality for all, which condition of society is the only one which can draw out to the full the varying capacities of the citizens and make the most of the knowledge and skill of mankind, the gain of so many ages, and thus do away for ever with MAKESHIFT. (*AWS*, vol II p. 483)

His lecture on 'Communism' ends with a plea:

> ... since it is just these means in which the difficulty lies, I appeal to all socialists, while they express their feelings about them honestly and fearlessly, not to make a quarrel of it with those whose aim is one with theirs, because there is a difference of opinion between them about the usefulness of the details of the means... So let us forgive the mistakes that others make, even if we make none ourselves, and be at peace amongst ourselves, that we may the better make war upon the monopolist. (*Political Writings*, pp. 239-40)

Differences remain, but we must not cripple ourselves in self-destructive quarrels over them. I see no evidence in such passages that Morris ever asserted that, were he again active, these were methods *he himself would use*.

But this, after all, was the essential distinction, discussed above, which he expressed in his earlier letters to Mahon, Glasse, and Glasier before the split of 1888. As he became physically more remote from the labour movement in the mid-1890s, Morris's exhortations to socialist unity became somewhat more urgent; but this was a shift of emphasis, not a change of attitude; even in the 1880s, friends and fellow socialists such as Scheu and Lane had criticised him as too willing to be put upon, too pacific and conciliatory.

As early as 1884, Morris embodied the fundamental view to which he continued to adhere in a cogent brief fable, which he published in *Justice*. (19 January, *AWS*, voL II pp. 114-16) The poultry of an entire country meet in solemn assembly (a parliament of fowls), and discuss the basic question of their condition, '*With what sauce shall we be eaten?*' After hours of energetic speeches, one ragged 'battered looking and middle-aged barn-door cock' rises and blurts out in a trembling, shrieking voice, 'In short, *I don't want to be eaten at all*: is it poss—?' but he is cut off by the others' cries of practical politics, municipal franchise, and so forth. The old cock withdraws, and the conclave passes a resolution, to be sent to the farmer's wife, which embodies their decision that 'while there were doubts as to the sauce to be used in the serving up, slow stewing was settled on as the least revolutionary form of cookery'. The tale's moral is an exhortation: 'Citizens, pray draw it for yourselves'. Once the moral was drawn, I believe, the 'middle-aged barn-door cock' remained true to it to the last.

Throughout his life, Morris's mind had renewed itself in interlocking cycles of creative effort and frustration. In each such cycle, he devoted arduous effort and massive attention to detail, confronted what he interpreted as failure or defeat, then turned with renewed intensity toward new, often larger, activities and endeavours. These enlarging cycles were subject to a kind of dialectic, in which aspects of each stage were re-expressed in later, modified forms. Periods in which more concrete or pragmatic aspects were dominant (creation of the Firm; Icelandic trips; formation of the Society for the Protection of Ancient Buildings; the political activity of the '80s) complemented and alternated with other periods of abstraction or introspection, in which he created highly intense and allegorical poetry, and the abstractions of his designs. Had this pattern continued, and Morris's health not deteriorated, he would have undertaken another cycle of social or political effort in the late 1890s. Who can guess what form this might have taken?

This first scene of Morris's utopian romance, *News from Nowhere*, could be directly from the *Socialist Diary*. The overwrought narrator leaves a faction-ridden meeting of the Socialist League and enters a carriage of the underground, 'that vapour bath of hurried and discontented humanity'. Self-reproachful because he cannot envision a new society, he thinks, 'If I could but see a day of it… if I could but see it.' (*CW*, vol.XVI p. 4) *News from Nowhere* can be read as a kind of infinite projection of these cyclical efforts to 'see it', and the *Diary* as a record of Morris's efforts to carry out Ellen's admonition to Guest, at the end of *News from Nowhere*:

> Go back again, now you have seen us, and your outward eyes have learned that in spite of all the infallible maxims of your day there is yet a time of rest in store for the world, when mastery has changed into fellowship — but not before… Go on… striving, with whatsoever pain and labour needs must be, to build up little by little the new day of fellowship, and rest, and happiness. (*CW*, vol. XVI pp. 210-11)

Morris's descriptions of a future society represent the contemplative aspect of his creative middle-age, and the *Diary* its active counterpart, the struggle to create fellowship and happiness in a real world.

Florence S. Boos
Cambridge, Massachusetts 1981

Acknowledgements

Even a modest editorial project such as this is inevitably a co-operative endeavour. I wish first to thank the two persons who contributed most to the preparation of the *Diary*, Stan Shipley and Bill Boos. As an editor of the *History Workshop Journal*, Stan was extraordinarily patient and gracious with many suggestions for the notes, maps, and introduction, and with materials from his own research; Stan and Mary Shipley's warm hospitality also lightened our visits to England. My husband Bill Boos first encouraged my interest in the *Diary*, discussed its substance with me many times, and worked through each draft of the notes and introduction.

I also owe special thanks to Ed and Ruth Frow of the Working-Class Movements Library, Old Trafford, Manchester, for their unusual hospitality and access to their private collection of socialist materials, and to Ronald Goldstein of Oxford, who was especially generous with information on the Socialist League, notes of League Conferences, and other records not readily available in Britain.

I would further like to thank the many people who answered queries promptly and thoroughly, and provided useful material for the textual and biographical notes. The following people helped particularly with the history of anarchism:

- Nicolas Walter of the Rationalist Press, who provided useful references and information on Frank Kitz and Charlotte Wilson;
- M.W.H. Schreuder, Head of the Department Britain–North America, International Institute for Social History, Amsterdam; and
- Edward Weber, Head, Labadie Collection, University of Michigan Library.

I would also like to express my appreciation to:

- Daniel Cameron, Paisley Central Library, Local History Department, for information about Robert Cochrane; to
- R.C. Kenedy, Assistant Keeper of the Library, Victoria and Albert Museum, for information about A.S. Cole; to
- C. Wilkins-Jones, Norfolk County Local Studies Librarian, for information about Fred Henderson; to
- Ken John of Essex, for information about Sam Mainwaring; to
- Ken Weller of London, for information about James Tochatti; to

- Judith Oppenheimer, Castle Howard Archivist, for access to Morris family correspondence with George and Rosalind Howard; and to
- Norah Gillow, Keeper, and Jill Halliwell, Assistant Keeper of the William Morris Gallery, for making available Morris's correspondence with Bruce Glasier.

Richard Lloyd-Jones, Frederick McDowell, Valerie Lagorio, and Alexander Kern of the Department of English at the University of Iowa aided and encouraged me while I worked on the *Diary*. Elinor L. Saunders assisted with travel to England, and Kim Merker of the Windhover Press made helpful comments on the preparation of the text for an earlier, limited edition of the *Diary*. R.C.H. Briggs, Head of the Board of Trustees, William Morris Centre, and Joan South, Honorary Secretary of the William Morris Society, helped me during my two stays at the William Morris House.

Finally, I am very grateful to the Bunting Institute of Radcliffe College, which provided support during the period of final preparation of the notes and introduction; and to the graduate College of the University of Iowa, which awarded two summer grants which facilitated research in England and a generous financial grant which assisted in the publication of this edition. The Society of Antiquaries has kindly given permission for the publication of the *Diary*, and the British Library, Victoria and Albert Museum, and William Morris Gallery provided the photographs which appear in the text.

My limited attempt to document three months of Morris's political activity has given rise to a year of work, hundreds of letters and interviews, and several thousand miles of travel. Even so, many uncomplete or inadequate entries remain. Everything I've uncovered has increased my respect for the stubborn foresight of the *Diary*'s pioneers of communism, anarchists and socialists who struggled with all their mental and physical substance to create a more humane society for their descendants. I hope this publication of the *Diary* will help recreate some of Morris's wholehearted contribution to their efforts.

Conventions and abbreviations

The text of the Socialist Diary may be found in British Museum Add. MS. 45,335, F.1-51. I have followed the example of Eugene LeMire's *The Unpublished Lectures of William Morris* and retained Morris's own punctuation. His use of colons and semicolons in place of periods often gives clauses a rhythmic evenness which suggests rapid and vigorous thought. The usage is not always consistent, but it seems arbitrary to differentiate between infelicitous 'errors' and purposefully unconventional usage. Likewise I have left intact his capitalisation, but small numerals have been written out, misspellings regularised according to nineteenth-century British usage, apparent writing errors excised, and abbreviations written out in square brackets.

The following abbreviations have been used in the notes:

M   William Morris

CW   *The Collected Works of William Morris*, Longmans, London 1910-15

Cw   *Commonweal*

AWS   May Morris, ed., *William Morris Artist Writer Socialist*, Oxford 1936

IISH   Amsterdam, International Institute of Social History

Kelvin *The Collected Letters of William Morris*, ed. Norman Kelvin. 4 vols. Princeton University Press, 1984-96.

Arnot   R. Page Arnot, *William Morris: The Man and the Myth*, Lawrence and Wishart, 1964

Glasier   J. Bruce Glasier, *William Morris and the Early Days of the Socialist Movement*, Longmans, London 1921

LeM Cal 'Appendix I: A Calendar of William Morris's Platform Career', in Eugene D. LeMire, *The Unpublished Lectures of William Morris*, Wayne State Univ., Detroit 1969

LeM Ch 'Appendix II: A Bibliographical Checklist of Morris's Speeches and Lectures', in LeMire, above

Quail John Quail, *The Slow Burning Fuse*, Granada, London 1978

Sharp and Marsh Frank C. Sharp and Jan Marsh, eds. *The Collected Letters of Jane Morris*, Boydell Press, Woodbridge, 2012.

Thompson *William Morris: Romantic to Revolutionary*, 2nd ed. Pantheon, New York 1977

WMorris Gal William Morris Gallery, Walthamstow

BL   British Library

OED   Oxford English Dictionary

May Morris with musical instrument
(Courtesy of the William Morris Gallery)

Returning to Morris's *Socialist Diary*

When in 1973 I first visited the British Library Manuscripts Room, I was overwhelmed to find some dozens of notebooks in Morris's handwriting, among which lay several unpublished literary, political and personal writings. Especially intriguing was a nondescript ruled notebook containing a fifty-one-page diary of Morris's socialist activities from 8 January–26 April 1887 written in his clear fair copy hand, with sections marked for deletion in a future printed version. Fresh from the events of the Vietnam War era, with its campus and draft protests, repeated student strikes, police and military interventions, and fraught electoral campaigns, I had no difficulty in anticipating that Morris's spirited and candid view of his socialist activities would contain observations of literary, historical, and personal interest.

In due course the *Diary* was published, but these editions have passed into history, and after more than three decades several entries needed updating, especially as the Socialist League Archives at the International Institute for Social History in Amsterdam have now been made available online. I was therefore pleased when the proprietor of Five Leaves Publications in Nottingham invited me to prepare a revised version of the *Diary*, offering a rare lifetime opportunity to rethink my earlier conclusions.

Although I haven't changed greatly in my evaluation of the *Diary*'s contents, here I would like to comment more broadly on the purposes which the *Diary* served for Morris during this period, his major preoccupations at the time, his qualified views on the immediate prospects for socialism, and why, though prepared carefully for the printer, the *Diary* was never published at the time. And finally, I would like to consider briefly once again Morris's controversial view that an effective socialist movement must above all maintain a non-legislative component, independent of political compromise and devoted to education and direct democracy. What prompted these views, and can anything be said in their favour?

1. What purposes were served by the *Diary*?

On 9 March 1887 Morris wrote to his daughter Jenny, 'I am writing a diary which may one day be published as a kind of view of the Socialist movement seen from the inside, Jonah's view of the whale, you know, my dear.' As the editor of *Commonweal*, Morris had written and inserted into its pages four prior such accounts of socialist campaigns in the preceding year,[1] but as we shall see, the 1887 *Diary* was different: longer, fraught with painful as well as hopeful assessments, and never published. Morris had seldom kept a diary in earlier life (the sole exception had been his Icelandic Journals of 1871 and 1873), and this one straddles the public and private constraints of a genre requiring both honest self-criticism and explanations suitable for a reading audience.

As such, the *Diary* served many purposes. It permitted Morris to jot down initial thoughts on ideas later written up in *Commonweal* as 'Notes on Passing Events' and editorial 'leading' essays—as well as the longer articles written and delivered during this period, such as 'Monopoly'[2] and his share of the co-authored serial, 'Socialism from the Root Up'.[3] Most of the topics of his other writings during the period—low wages, unemployment, harsh legal judgments, police attacks on socialists, Irish Home Rule, the Paris Commune celebration, party divisions and votes in Parliament, the proposed construction of a railway which would deface the Lake District, mining agitation in north England and Scotland, and his views on desirable priorities for socialists—appear also in the *Diary*.

Conversely, a more personal venue may have permitted Morris occasional relief from the need to frame every observation into a public statement. He was free in its pages to veer off the immediate topic—to comment on his admiration for a medieval Flemish tapestry newly purchased by the Victoria and Albert Museum (26 January), remark on the pleasure of translating the *Odyssey* (3 February), discuss his health or family's travel plans, vent irritation at the rudeness, ineptitude, or combativeness of various fellow socialists (3 March, 9 March), or brood privately over obstacles to future socialist success. As the parliamentarian (mostly state-socialist leaning) and anti-parliamentarian (mostly anarcho-communist and 'collectivist'-anarchist leaning) factions in the Socialist League

---

[1] 'A Report from the Provinces,' April; 'Socialism in Dublin and Yorkshire,' May; 'A Letter from Scotland,' 3 July; 'The Sequel of the Scotch Letter,' 10 July.

[2] The probable first date of delivery for 'Monopoly' was 20 February 1887, and it was delivered twenty times. See LeMire, Cal., 309.

[3] 'Socialism from the Root Up' ran in *Commonweal* from 15 May 1886–19 May 1888.

became ever less willing to compromise, eventually leading to a major split in August 1888, Council meetings and League business in general became a considerable strain, and the *Diary* records that, though resolute as always, Morris felt backed into a corner on many occasions.

The *Diary* also permitted him to remark honestly on the impoverished condition of many in his audiences as well as their limited ability to absorb his remarks. His observations on the low responsiveness of his London area audiences, as opposed to his northern ones, show consistent regret:

> [Merton Abbey SL] they have been very badly off there this winter and there is little to wonder at in their discontent; but with a few exceptions they have not yet learned what Socialism means... . [25 January]

> [Hammersmith Radical Club] I thought the applause rather hollow as the really radical part of the audience... were quite untouched by Socialism: they seemed to me a very discouraging set of men; but perhaps can be got at somehow. [26 January]

> [Mitcham SL] they were very quiet and attentive... but I doubt if most of them understood anything I said... I wonder sometimes if people will remember in times to come to what a depth of degradation the ordinary English workman has been reduced; I felt very downcast amongst these poor people in their poor hutch whose opening I attended some three months back (and they were rather proud of it)... . Yet I felt as if I might be doing some good there: the branch is making way amongst a most wretched population. [23 February]

> [Chiswick Hall Club] ['Monopoly'] was a new lecture, and good, though I say it, and I really did my best; but they hung on my hands as heavy as lead. [21 March]

> [Hackney Club]... the audience was civil and inclined to agree, but I couldn't flatter myself that they mostly understood me, simple as the lecture was. [30 March][4]

On the other hand, some of Morris's London lectures were well-received, and several drew substantial audiences; he notes of a Peckham High

---

[4] See also remarks in entries for 15 January, 26 January, 7 February, 9 March, and 21 March.

Street meeting on 12 February that 'a good part of the audience (not a large one about one hundred I should think...), was quite enthusiastic.' More gratifyingly, his northern trips were highly successful; on 21 March he reported that an Edinburgh audience was 'both attentive and very enthusiastic... . In fact things seem on the rise in Scotland... : best of all the general feeling of advanced political people is turning our way there.' The high point of the *Diary* was his report of an April tour of mining districts, where in Glasgow he spoke to an indoor audience of 1000 and at Newcastle to a huge outdoor crowd of many thousands, who 'listened intently and were heartily with us' [27 April].

Nonetheless, preaching socialism was uphill work, and moreover the signs of misery Morris encountered in his travels angered and depressed him. He recorded carefully the exact circumstances of a Newcastle strike, as recounted by a miner: 'the men were working about four days a week and only earning... about thirteen s[hillings], and the masters are for reducing their wages by twelve and a half per cent... although according to the sliding scale of wages agreed to by employers and employed this was not called for...' [27 April] The *Commonweal* of the period contains many sarcastic barbs against those who enforced or rationalized such conditions: the 29 January 'Notes on Passing Events' records the case of a workhouse inmate imprisoned for failure to perform manual labour on a diet of hot water and dry bread; and when a parliamentary commission asserted the comparatively good position of English workers, Morris counters sharply: 'Will the Commissioners... say where in Europe or Asia they can find a workman more miserably pinched and resourceless than the south-west country labourer with his income of 10s a-week when things are going well?' [29 January] When an inquest into the demise of two children in nearby Chiswick reported their deaths as caused by living in a 'vitiated atmosphere', Morris exclaims, 'I suppose these victims of vitiated atmosphere will not be set among the record of those who were starved to death? (I have not patience to remember the euphemism for that), but starved to death they were.' [19 February]

2. What were Morris's major *political* preoccupations during this period?

Morris's many fulminations against politics *per se*, both in his essays and in *News from Nowhere* (where the new society is allegedly free of politics — that is, of factionalism) may have obscured the extent to which he was a political junkie. Each day he read the *Daily News* – and apparently other papers on occasion. He followed closely its fiery anti-imperialist and reformist editorials,[5] which at times resemble Morris's own writings in his emergent pre-Socialist phase. If Morris's relationship with his former political affiliation, the Gladstonian wing of the Liberal Party, might be described as an intense love-hate relationship, one might term his response to the anti-Tory, pro-Home Rule, but anti-Socialist *Daily News* as a running lovers' quarrel. He studied each issue of the *News* with care and framed the predictions and sarcastic ripostes of his *Commonweal* columns in response. More than a hundred years later these short, pithy commentaries still make excellent and often amusing reading — a higher-order analogue of tweeting, perhaps. Presumably his 'Notes on News' were directed at *Commonweal* readers who might not otherwise be able or choose to afford a newspaper, and they help make *Commonweal* more current, timely, and immediately relevant than other socialist or anarchist papers of the period such as *Justice*, *Liberty*, or *Freedom*.

Along with his fellow socialists Morris was offended by the repeated arrests and imprisonment of socialist speakers, as recorded in the *Diary*. In a period in which a high proportion of the population lacked effective literacy, street preaching was necessary to spread the message of socialism. Nonetheless, the running battle between socialist speakers and the police took a heavy toll in arrests and fines. At one point Morris interrupts the *Diary*'s narrative to remark:

> I may note here for the benefit of well-to-do West Enders that the police are incredibly rough and brutal to the poor people in the East End; and that they treated [James] Allman very ill. (23 February)

(Allman, a tailor's assistant, had been sentenced to a month in prison after a testimony in which he pointed out the bias of the authorities in arresting only socialist speakers.) Morris himself had been arrested in September 1885 when attending the trial of several socialists arraigned for speaking at an open-air site at Dod Street in the East End. Among those sentenced was Lewis Lyons, a tailor and member of the Socialist Democratic

---

[5]   Its editor through 1886 was Frank Harrison Hill; little seems known about Hill, but his editorials against British interventionism do bear similarities to Morris's own rhetoric from the period. In 1887 John Robinson became titular editor, with the actual editing delegated to Peter William Clayden, a former Unitarian minister. The relationship between Morris and the *Daily News* merits further investigation.

Federation, to whom the judge delivered a sentence of two months hard labour. When Morris and his fellow socialists inside the courtroom shouted 'Shame!' Morris was promptly arrested and charged with attacking an officer; he too would doubtless have been sentenced had the judge not been apprised of his literary status. Only six months after the *Diary*'s close, on 13 November 1887, Morris was also present at the event later known as 'Bloody Sunday', in which the police and army attacked those attending a mass meeting at Trafalgar Square called by the SDF and the Irish National League, at which 400 were arrested and 200 reportedly injured. Worse happened the next week, however, when the opposing parties regrouped and an even larger police force charged on free-speech protesters at the same location, fatally wounding at least two men. The first to die of injuries was Alfred Linnell, and an immense audience gathered to hear Morris deliver the latter's funeral oration and join in singing a poem composed by Morris for the occasion, 'A Death Song':

> Here lies the sign that we shall break our prison;
> Amidst the storm he won a prisoner's rest;
> But in the cloudy dawn the sun arisen
> Brings us our day of work to win the best.
> *Not one, not one, nor thousands must they slay*
> *But one and all if they would dusk the day.*

Morris himself nonetheless repeatedly advised caution and strategic avoidance of situations which could lead to arrests, causing pain to those imprisoned and sapping the League's resources. The *Diary* records his criticisms of the rival SDF's attempts to promote shows of force, and on March 3rd he remarked wearily of a League Council meeting: 'A good deal of talk about the open-air-free-speech business: we are to have it out next Monday, when I shall take some trouble to get them to be reasonable but don't expect to succeed.' He had explained his position the preceding August in a letter to Bruce Glasier:

> You will see that we are in hot water again with the police here, and for my part I think it a great nuisance. It is after all a side issue, and I grudge everything that takes people's attention off the true economical and social issues which are the only things of importance…. (16 August 1886, Kelvin 2:565-66)

Apart from these urgent practical matters, however, a study of his *Commonweal* writings and the *Diary* would seem to indicate that few causes interested Morris more deeply than Irish Home Rule. Morris had come to political maturity in a period of Liberal Party dominance, but in 1886 this majority was reversed, with the anti-Home Rule Liberal Unionists splitting from the Gladstonian Liberals and small Irish Parliamentary Party to throw the balance of power to the Conservatives. Morris evaluated each shift in parliamentary coalitions from the perspective of Home Rule, angry at attempts by the Liberal Unionists to pull the Liberals from their earlier stated support for Irish independence, frustrated at Gladstone's willingness to dump his signature reform policy, offended by the churning debates which resulted in a further harsh Coercion Bill for Ireland (the Criminal Law and Procedures Act of 1887), and irritated with the Irish parliamentary leaders who advocated pro-landlord policies, thus attempting to reduce non-land-holding farmers into a permanent class of serfs.

In 1886 Morris had visited Dublin on a speaking tour, during 1886–87 he published four *Commonweal* articles and numerous shorter discussions of Irish affairs,[6] and in 1887 he spoke at three demonstrations against the Coercion Bill for Ireland, one of which had been organized by the Socialist League and a second by its close ally, the London Labour Emancipation League.[7] Clearly Morris saw Irish Home Rule as a moral issue:

> [The Coercion Bill] is… felt to be what the *Pall Mall* called it the other evening, a declaration of war against Ireland;… and if [the Irish people] had, I will not say any chance of success, but any opportunity, they would make that manifest by rising in armed revolt against the central tyranny, and to a large part at least of the peoples of England, Scotland, and Wales, that rebellion seems a righteous one; to how large a portion no general election will make clear to us, but rather the march of events. [9 April]

---

6   'Independent Ireland,' 1 May 1886; 'Home Rule or Humbug,' 26 June 1886; 'The Law in Ireland,' 25 December 1886; and 'Law and Order in Ireland,' 9 April 1887.

7   These were held on 13 April, 21 May, and 25 September. Morris discusses the Home Rule debates in his 9 March *Diary* entry but, perhaps due to a gap between 30 March and 27 April, the 13 April meeting is not described. Several issues may have been promoted at a single meeting; for example, the demonstrations in favour of 'Free Speech' may have included mention of the repression of free speech for Ireland.

Here, as often, the ever-embattled Morris was nonetheless optimistic about the speed of that 'march', since a modified Home Rule bill was not passed until 1912, only to be deferred and negated by a world war. But 130 years after Morris's remarks — after 'the Troubles', a Revolution, fission, guerilla warfare, religious murders, and repeated conflicts — most recently over Brexit — it is hard to dismiss his belief in the urgent need for Irish independence (and unity) as a mere peripheral concern.

Possibly the ineffectuality of the Irish wing of Parliament also influenced Morris's views on the issue of 'parliamentarianism', that is, on whether the Socialist League should run candidates for the current English parliament. Minority representation within the governing body of Great Britain had been helpless to promote Irish interests. Why not instead campaign for an alternate government entirely, a People's Parliament after the model of the hoped-for independent National Parliament for Ireland—Home Rule for the People, as it were? This was the model of the 'Committees of Public Safety' utilised by revolutionary patriots at the onset of the American and French Revolutions, and, of more immediate interest to Morris, by the Paris Communards. Like these antecedents, in *News from Nowhere* 'Committees of Public Safety' form a shadow rising government which administers supplies and maintains public order until at last popular sentiment entirely delegitimises the former ruling classes.

In part due to Morris's influence, the Socialist League was the most international of Britain's several socialist bodies of the 1880s. Morris served as League delegate to socialist congresses in both France and Germany, and the *Diary* records his contacts with several socialist and anarchist emigrés of the day, most notably Henry Charles (German), Victor Dave (French), Peter Kropotkin (Russian), and his close friend Andreas Scheu (German).[8] At the inauguration of *Commonweal* he had begun a serial poem on the Communard struggle — his first and only epic devoted to a post-medieval topic, 'The Pilgrims of Hope', serialized between February 1885 and May 1886, and Eugene LeMire's checklist of Morris's speeches records four addresses at the annual pan-socialist Paris Commune celebrations, in 1885, 1887, 1888, and 1890. Morris had

---

[8] As a member of the SDF 1883–84, Morris had strongly disapproved of what he considered Hyndman's prejudice against foreigners. He wrote to Robert Thomson on 1 January 1885, describing Hyndman: 'Hence attacks on foreigners as foreigners, or at least sneers at them; conquetting also with jingoism in various forms…' (Kelvin 2:368; cf. Thompson, 342-43, 363)

written to Jenny on 17 March 1887 that he feared he would have nothing new to say on the matter at that evening's Commune celebration — 'for though it is proper & right to celebrate the day, one has by now said all that one has to say on the subject'[9] — but he did.

For Morris personally, the history of this event was a reminder that even death might be required of professing socialists such as himself: 'with the chance of bodily sacrifice close a-head there come also times of trial which either raise a man to the due tragic pitch or cast him aside as a useless and empty vapourer.'[10] More centrally, the Communards' struggle had served two purposes: it had shown that mere 'ordinary' people could rise to heroism for their cause, and it heralded the possibility of a future and more successful revolt. Neither of these could be assumed without some leap of faith. Morris argued that not only had the more noted French Communards willingly sacrificed all for their cause, but so also had the unknown masses: 'who can doubt that the nameless multitude who died so heroically had sacrificed day by day other things than life, before it came to that?' Similarly, it might seem hopeless to expect an uprising of those who formed 'the enormous mass of people so degraded by their circumstances that they can scarcely understand any hope for their redemption,' — British workers, that is — but like their humble Communard counterparts, these too may rise:

> The revolution itself will raise those for whom the revolution must be made. Their newborn hope translated into action will develop their human and social qualities, and the struggle itself will fit them to receive the benefits of the new life which revolution will make possible for them. It is for boldly seizing the opportunity offered for thus elevating the mass of the workers into heroism that we now celebrate the men of the Commune of Paris. ['Why We Celebrate the Commune of Paris,' 19 March]

This intractable chicken-and-egg problem — how to stir the truly immiserated into action — would continue to preoccupy Morris and his fellow socialists until the end of his century and well beyond. Precisely because it was a failed struggle, Morris argues, the Paris Commune can serve as a precedent:

---

9 Kelvin, *Letters*, 2, 627-28.
10 Morris's essay appeared two days after the Commune celebration in the *Commonweal* for 19 March 1887.

> ... if to-day any one doubts that they were fighting for the
> emancipation of labour, their enemies at the time had no doubt
> about the matter. They saw in them no mere political opponents,
> but 'enemies of society', people who could not live in the same
> world with them, because the basis of their ideas of life was
> different—to wit, humanity, not property. This was why the fall
> of the Commune was celebrated... by such a riot of blood and
> cruelty on the part of the conquerors as quite literally has no
> parallel in modern times. And it is by that same token that we
> honour them as the foundation-stone of the new world that is
> to be. [Ibid.]

Morris had just completed a revolutionary prose romance for *Commonweal*, *A Dream of John Ball*, serialized from 13 November 1886–22 January 1887, with the final two numbers overlapping the period of the *Diary*. In this — perhaps Morris's finest treatment of the socialists' painful problem of deferred hopes — a time traveller from the present day returns to visit with the revolutionary peasant-priest John Ball, about to be executed for his part in the Peasant's Revolt of 1381. Ball is aghast to learn from his reluctantly truthful visitor that even in a later (capitalistic) economic order, men will still not be free. Morris's narrator can only assure him that his sacrifice will not be vain, for those of this later century will at least understand and struggle against their plight. Even in 1887, however, he can predict neither the time nor the means: 'The time will come, John Ball, when that dream of thine that this shall one day be, shall be a thing that men shall talk of soberly, and as a thing soon to come about, [Morris's own day]... therefore, hast thou done well to hope it;... Yet shall all bring about the end, till thy deeming of folly and ours shall be one, and thy hope and our hope; and then—the Day will have come.'[11]

3. What did Morris think were the prospects for socialism?

As we have seen, Morris practised a disciplined 'pessimism of the intellect, optimism of the will.' The *Diary* may represent a transitional period in his assessment of future possibilities, as the difficulties of inspiring working people to grasp the ideals of shared control of resources were every day manifest to him. During 1887 and later he struggled to convince others of the need for widespread advocacy rather

---

[11] CW 16, 286.

than immediate campaigning. Electioneering would become the final end and goal of supposed socialists, he argued; at best as a tiny minority their delegates would become absorbed in the larger corrupted body, and at worst, they would adopt its corrupting practices, as he wrote to John Glasse in May of that year:

> I believe that the Socialists will certainly send members to Parliament when they are strong enough to do so: in itself I see no harm in that, so long as [they are not] prepared by passing palliative measures to keep 'Society' alive. But I fear that many of them will be drawn into that error by the corrupting influence of a body professedly hostile to Socialism: and therefore... I think it will be necessary always to keep alive a body of Socialists of principle who will refuse responsibility for the actions of the parliamentary portion of the party...[12]

At least one wing of the socialist movement should devote itself to promoting this broader vision: 'I think the duty of the League is educational entirely at present; and that duty is all the more important since the SDF has entirely given up that side of things.'[13] Moreover, a change in public perception must precede any great social shift, as he would argue in his 1890 essay 'Communism':

> Our business... is the making of Socialists, i. e., convincing people that Socialism is good for them and is possible. When we have enough people of that way of thinking they will find out what action is necessary for putting their principles in practice. Until we have that mass of opinion, action for a general change that will benefit the whole people is *impossible*. Have we that body of opinion or anything like it? Surely not. If we look outside that glamour, that charmed atmosphere of party warfare in which we necessarily move, we shall see this clearly: that though there are a great many who believe it possible to compel their masters by some means or another to behave better to them, and though they are prepared to compel them (by so-called peaceful means, strikes and the like), all but a very small minority are not prepared *to do without masters*... When they are so prepared, then Socialism will be realized; but nothing can push it on a day in advance of that time.[14]

---

[12]   23 May, 1887, Kelvin 2:658.

[13]   Letter to Joseph Lane, 30 March 1887, Kelvin 2:631, BL 45,345.

[14]   'Communism,' in Morton, *Political Writings*, 225.

One can argue for some of the pragmatic aspects of Morris's position. The Socialist League was already stretched thin in defending against police attacks its program of outreach through street lectures — an effort necessary for reaching a semi-illiterate audience in a pre-digital age. This, in addition to their other activities such as lectures, protests, maintaining outlying branches, and the distribution of *Commonweal*, was exhausting, and it is more than remarkable that so small a band of adherents managed as much as they did; had they had attempted more, arguably they might also have achieved less on other fronts. Moreover, as those who have engaged in losing causist political campaigns can testify, these are resource-intensive and discouraging at best, even prompting derision and backlash. Electors were a selective middle-class minority of Britain's inhabitants, scarcely motivated to overthrow their own dominance; not surprisingly the SDF's two London candidates in the 1885 election had together polled less than sixty votes. The first socialist electoral success would not occur until 1891, when the Fabian Sidney Webb was elected a member of the London County Council.

And though the views of parliamentary socialists such as Friedrich Engels and Eleanor Marx have been well-remembered, a study of the Socialist League London membership more broadly suggests that in the late 1880s its anarchist-leaning wing was equally or nearly as powerful as the collectivist/parliamentary group, and thus no set of tactics or compromises might have avoided internal division. Morris was also attached to Andreas Scheu, Joseph Lane, Claus Henry Mordhurst, James Tochatti, John Carruthers, Emery Walker, Charles Faulkner, Philip Webb, and other League members less attracted to parliamentary campaigns, many of whom were personal friends or members of his own Hammersmith Branch; and although his views differed from those of Britain's chief anarchist theorist, Peter Kropotkin, the two men seem to have exerted a reciprocal influence on one another. Morris also found some of the collectivists personally repellent (Hyndman, Aveling, Donald), and since those he disliked seem to have also irritated or angered comrades who otherwise agreed with their views,[15] his reactions should not be dismissed as entirely motivated by bias.

---

[15] As discussed above, Hyndman was seen as over-controlling, and accused of condescension to workers and émigrés, who of course formed a large proportion of socialists; Donald later joined but was expelled from the Independent Labour Party. Aveling was known for his irritating habit of borrowing from fellow socialists much poorer than he and refusing repayment.

More personally, by background and experience (for example, in his work for the Society for the Protection of Ancient Buildings) Morris was superbly fitted for the role which he advocated: that of 'preaching and teaching' to 'make Socialists'.[16] The modern editor of his essays for *Justice* and *Commonweal*, Nicholas Salmon, offers a testimony to Morris's work for the socialist movement:

> Between 1883 and 1890 he was probably the most active propagandist in the whole country. In a seven year period he addressed over 1,000 meetings and was heard in person by as many as 250,000 people. His articles and editorials reached thousands more. As [E.P.] Thompson has written '... every group of Socialists included some who had been converted by his words...' His lecture campaign of 1883 to 1890 remains one of the most impressive ever undertaken by a British politician.[17]

Yet pragmatic concerns were not those which most influenced Morris. As we have seen, his interpretation of history suggested that revolutions often resulted from concerted collective action, not party politics. Neither could he benefit from the hindsight afforded twenty-first century historians, who can adduce both recent violent anti-democratic revolutions (e.g. in Russia and Germany) as well as the rise of electorally-created relatively social democratic governments. Like Marx, Morris believed that capitalism (what he called 'commercialism') would fall of its own pyramidal excesses — that is, as capitalists (in modern terminology, the .001%) came to control most of the world's resources, the workers (the 99.999%) would be forced to rebel. A slight distribution of these resources downwards ('trickle down') would create a client class of managers and parasites — the various ranks of the bourgeoisie — and thus merely increase the capitalists' power of further engorgement.[18] As

---

[16] 'Communism,' in Morton, *Political Writings*, 225. When in July 1884 he was pressed by Andreas Scheu to assume a position of greater leadership in the SDF, Morris had demurred on the grounds that: '[M]y habits are quiet & studious and if I am too much worried with 'politics' ie intrigue, I shall be no use to the Cause as a writer.' (18 July, Kelvin 2:300)

[17] Salmon, *Political Writings: Contributions to* Justice *and* Commonweal *1883–1890*, Bristol, Thoemmes Press, 1994, xlvi, xlviii. The citation is from Thompson, 602. In his youth Morris had edited the *Oxford and Cambridge Magazine*, which strongly promoted worker and outreach education.

[18] Like Marx, he believed the need to exploit foreign markets by force was a sign of the instability of the competitive system, 'the agony of capitalism

he argued later in the same year: 'at present when the rights of capital are admitted and all that is claimed is a proportional share in the profits, it means a kind of relief to the employers, an additional poor-rate levied from the workers...'[19]

Though Morris had studied Marx, these views were also his own, reached independently from personal experience. I have argued elsewhere[20] that they derived in part from a deep and seldom-acknowledged source. At an early opportunity Morris had removed himself from financial and personal associations with the source of his family's original wealth, the Devonshire Great Consolidated Copper Mining Company, but he cannot have been unaware of its operations. This mine fought its workers ruthlessly for years, repeatedly lowering their wages on the grounds of a need to remain competitive in world markets. It maintained a helpless client union forced into steady retreat throughout the 1870s and '80s, and finally collapsed entirely under the pressure of foreign competition. In short, as Morris would argue, capitalism *required* the exploitation of workers, internecine conflicts within the different ranks of workers, and predatory reciprocal assaults of capitalists on one another. A society of such 'commercial war' was itself both exponentially destructive and ultimately doomed. Morris argued in Foucauldian fashion that 'while this commercial war lasts we are all the slaves of it,'[21] since both the dispossessed and possessing classes must fight for market survival. The only solution to this collective madness, he argued in 'Socialism', delivered many times between June 1885 and November 1887, was an entirely new basis for society, that of equality:

---

driven by a force it cannot resist to seek for new & ever new markets... .'
(1885 'Commercial War,' ed. Florence Boos, *Journal of Pre-Raphaelite Studies* 19 [Winter 2010], 61.

[19] 'The Policy of Abstention,' *AWS* II, 443, delivered on 30 July and 24 August 1887. Moreover, 'they are invited to vote and take some part in government in order that they may help their rulers to find out what must be conceded, and what may be refused to the workers; and to give an appearance of freedom of action to them.'

[20] Florence Boos and Patrick O'Sullivan,'Morris's Socialism and the Devonshire Great Consols,' *Journal of William Morris Studies*, 20.1 (Spring 2012): 11-39. http://www.morrissociety.org/publications/JWMS/
http:// http:victorianfboos.studio.uiowa.edu/Devonshire.2012.pdf

[21] 'Commercial War,' 46.

> The aim of socialism is to make the best by man's effort of the chances of happiness which the life of man upon the earth offers us,… and to assure to everyone born into the world his full share of that chance: and this can only be assured to him by men combining together for this benefit:… . We want to make people leave off saying[,] this is mine and that is thine, and to say[,] this is ours.[22]

By the 1890s, like many other contemporary socialists, Morris had accepted the likelihood that any revolution in social circumstances would be deferred. Moreover, though he hoped, he was not certain that this end could be attained by peaceful means.

> … the idea of successful insurrection within a measurable distance of time is only [in] the heads of the anarchists, who seem to have a strange notion that even equality would not be acceptable if [it] were not gained by violence only. Almost everyone has ceased to believe in the change coming by catastrophe.

> Well, since the battle has been made a matter of commerce, and the God of War must now wear a mantle of bank-notes and wear a crown of guineas,… since war has been commercialized, I say, we shall… not be called upon to gain our point by battle in the field.[23]

Yet the issue of the unpreparedness of the workers obtruded again: how can the workers as presently constituted lead a peaceful and socialist revolution? He had identified this problem in his 1888 lecture, 'Equality'.[24]

> [T]hough the workers are more useful than the idlers, yet they too are corrupted and degraded by their position. No one can expect to find the virtues of free men in slaves. No[,] if the present state of Society merely breaks up without a conscious effort at transformation, the end[,] the fall of Europe[,] may be long in coming, but when it does come it will be far more terrible[,] far more confused and full of suffering than the period of the fall of Rome.

---

[22] 'Socialism,' ed. Florence Boos, *Journal of William Morris Studies* 18.4 (Winter 2010), 29-30.

[23] 'What We Have to Look For', *Journal of William Morris Studies*, 18.4 (2010), 44-45, 42, delivered 31 March 1895.

[24] Delivered eight times from 30 Sept 1888 to 9 February 1890, *Journal of Pre-Raphaelite Studies*, 20 (spring 2011), 53.

He still felt apprehension in 1895, shortly before his death, as expressed in 'What We Have To Look For'.

> I have thought the matter up and down and in and out, and I cannot for the life of me see how the great change which we long for can come otherwise than by disturbance and suffering of some kind.[25]

Prescient? This was an unresolved dilemma which Morris had continued to ponder in nuanced and varied forms over the nine years between the *Diary* and his death.

4. Why was the *Diary* never published?

A list of Morris's activities during this short time is staggering — within this slightly-more-than-three-month period, we have seen that he managed a successful business, correspondence (forty letters of the period are preserved in Kelvin's *Collected Letters*), the completion of two significant literary works (*A Dream of John Ball* and 'The Pilgrims of Hope'), progress on a classical translation, extensive weekly reports and articles for *Commonweal*, Socialist League business, protests, lecture tours, outdoor preaching, and of course the *Diary* itself, and it is understandable that in the press of preparations for the annual Socialist League Conference held on 29 May 1887, Morris should have suspended the *Diary* and failed to issue it as originally planned.

It should be clear by now that some portion of its contents were also unsuitable for publication. If Morris expurgated honest accounts of the sharp divisions within the League or his frustrated remarks on the behaviour of colleagues — as his marks for excisions indicated that he intended to do — the results would be bland and misleading.[26] Most crucially, Morris could not wound the feelings of potential *Commonweal* readers by commenting on the low level of comprehension in his audiences — the very audiences at whom the newspaper was directed. But, as we have seen, the *Diary* served a purpose in providing a realm

---

[25] 'What We Have to Look For', 44.

[26] Among other things, his excisions remove mention of dissensions at Council meetings as well as all criticism of socialist speakers or branch meeting places. An electronic copy of the manuscript with excisions marked for the printer appears on the William Morris Archive, http://morrisedition.lib.uiowa.edu/diaries.html.

in which Morris could sort out his many thoughts and reactions; and an honesty and fullness unsuited to its immediate publication has made it more valuable to later audiences as a genuine 'Jonah's eye' view.

* * *

When I edited the *Diary* in 1980–81, no one could be found to sympathize with Morris's distrustful view of electoral politics, and I devoted much of my previous introduction to delineating the exact parameters of his carefully calibrated statements on this issue, differently nuanced but unchanged in its fundamentals over a fourteen-year period. I would not now claim that Morris succeeded in squaring the circle — solving the conundrum of how an oppressed group without power can seize control while retaining its original egalitarian aims — but at least he faced this issue with more insight into its essentially Catch-22 problematics than perhaps anyone of his era. Moreover, thirty-six years after my first introduction, it is not difficult to note parallels between the problems faced by nascent socialism in the late 1880s and the political impasses of Britain and the United States. In the UK an apparently democratic electoral process elevated New Labour and Tory governments, and most recently initiated the isolationist, anti-internationalist Brexit. The late Nicholas Salmon gave his views on his country's political situation in 1996:

> With the advantage of hindsight it is clear that [Morris's] worst fears have come true. After one hundred years of parliamentary representation we are no nearer the social revolution and, more significantly, the Labour Party now openly defends the system it was originally intended to destroy. Just as Morris predicted, the working classes are now leaderless as there is no effective extra-parliamentary body from which to continue the class struggle. Surely it is time we reassessed his political writings and considered their implications for our own age.[27]

In the United States, elections routinely elevate candidates openly tied to special interests, in a 'commercial war' against both equality and democratic norms. For Morris's perceived spectrum of Old Tories, Tories, Whigs/Liberal Unionists, Liberals, Radicals, and Socialists, read

---

[27] Salmon, Nicholas, intro., *Journalism: Contributions to* Commonweal *1885–1890*, Brighton: Thommes Press, 1996, xxxiii.

Alt-Right, Republicans, Establishment Democrats, would-be reformist Democrats, and those sceptical of the possibility of such reformation, entirely marginalized politically into third parties or lacking all representation. Yet even as the traditional political parties still appeal for support, we witness an upsurge of 'movements' — more, in fact, as a perceived political swamp overflows its banks — Black Lives Matter, Occupy, Standing Rock and Water Protectors, Sandy Hook Promise, 350.org, and other coalitions to defend the environment, immigrant rights, chemical-free food, or a world without war. In my own small Midwestern city, so many such groups have mushroomed recently that several websites and twitter feeds are devoted to coordinating their activities. My point is that social movements seem to flourish both within and outside the parameters of political parties, and so Morris may not have been entirely misguided to direct his energies elsewhere. This itself was no simple task, for as Morris stated in his 1887 speech on the Paris Commune, 'Truly it is harder to live for a cause than to die for it,'[28] an insight borne out by the events of his *Socialist Diary* and their continuing aftermath.

Florence S. Boos
June 2017
Iowa City, Iowa and Gibsons, British Columbia

---

[28] 'Why We Celebrate the Commune of Paris', *Commonweal*, 19 March 1887.

Publication note

The *Socialist Diary* was issued without notes in a limited fine press edition at the Windhover Press, 1981; with notes in the *History Workshop Journal* 13 (1982); and under separate cover with additions by the Journeyman Press and the London History Workshop Centre, 1985. I am grateful to Graham Seaman for his 2005 digitization of the *Socialist Diary* for Marxists.org, which has aided me in preparing this revised edition. I have also been able to expand the biographical information for this new edition through the generous help of labour historian Stephen Williams, who has devoted many hours to searching through census and newspaper records for information on Morris's lesser-known socialist comrades. And finally, Kimberly A. Maher, the Project Manager of the William Morris Archive, has helped in gathering and editing images.

William Morris 1884 (Courtesy of the Victoria and Albert Museum)

[I begin what may be called my diary from this point
January 25th 1887.]
I went down to lecture at Merton Abbey last Sunday: the
little room was pretty full of men mostly of the labourer
class: any thing attacking the upper classes directly moved
their enthusiasm; of their discontent there could be no doubt
or the sincerity of their class hatred: they have been very
badly off there ~~a~~ this winter, and there is little to wonder
at in their discontent; but with a few exceptions they
have not yet learned what Socialism means; they and
Frank Kitz were much excited about the Norwich affair*,
and ~~the~~ made a very hot speech: he was much exercised
about the police ~~being~~ all about the place, detectives
inside and so on: I fancy their game is to try to catch
the Club-serving ~~now~~ members with beer or in some way breaking
the law. But there is no doubt that there is a good
deal of stir amongst the labourers about there; the
place is wretchedly poor.
I slept at Merton, and in the morning got the Norwich
paper with a full account of the trial of Mowbray &
Henderson; the Judges summing up of the case was
amusing & ~~in~~ instructive, as showing a sort of survival
of the old sort of ~~kings of~~ bullying of the Castlereagh
times mixed with a ~~~~ grotesque attempt

Socialist Diary, first page (British Library Add MS 45,335)

The *Diary*

[I begin what may be called my diary from this point **January 25ᵗʰ, 1887**]

I went down to lecture at Merton Abbey[1] last Sunday: the little room was pretty full of men mostly of the labourer class: anything attacking the upper classes directly moved their enthusiasm; of their discontent there could be no doubt or the sincerity of their class hatred: they have been very badly off there this winter[2] and there is little to wonder at in their discontent; but with a few exceptions they have not yet learned what Socialism means; they and Frank Kitz were much excited about the Norwich affair*[3] and he made a very hot speech:[4] he was much exercised about the police being all

---

[1] Dissatisfied with commercial processes available for making Morris and Co. goods, Morris had established in 1881 a factory for colouring prints, wallpapers, and stained glass in unused buildings at Merton Abbey, on the banks of the river Wandle, in Surrey. During many visits, he helped found and maintain a branch of the SL; though the Merton branch announced weekly Thursday committee meetings and Sunday discussions, *Commonweal* reports seem to indicate that it was not one of the more active branches. On Sunday 23 January, Morris spoke on 'True and False Society', a familiar lecture delivered four times the preceding year, and later reprinted in *CW* vol. 23 pp. 215-37 (see LeMire Ch, p. 307 no. 90). LeMire Cal, p. 260 lists Morris as previously scheduled to deliver an evening speech at Cleveland Hall, Cleveland Street, London, so the *Diary* indicates a change in plans.

[2] Since it was largely tied to the precarious block-printing industry, the economy of the Merton area was heavily vulnerable to one of the severest depressions of the second half of the century, the Great Depression of 1886; this continued through the winter of 1886–87, began to recede slightly later in the year, and had finally lifted by 1890.

[3] On Friday 14 January, during a visit to Norwich, London SL members Charles Mowbray and Fred Henderson were arrested, after a crowd of unemployed to whom they had delivered speeches smashed windows en route to the Guildhall to demand relief. Henderson was sentenced to four months in prison, and Mowbray, married and the father of five children, received nine months. On 23 January, Kitz, M, and the Merton socialists would have just heard the news of their indictment at the previous day's assizes.

* The star Morris placed after 'Norwich affair' refers to the clipping of his letter on the subject to the *Daily News*, which he inserted facing the next page of his notebook. See footnote 9.

[4] Something of Frank Kitz's combative temperament may be reflected in the tone of the report he wrote for the 5 February *Commonweal* p 48, on events

about the place, detectives inside and so on: I fancy their game is to try to catch the club serving non-members with beer or in some way breaking the law.[5] But there is no doubt that there is a good deal of stir amongst the labourers about there; the place is wretchedly poor.

I slept at Merton, and in the morning got the Norwich paper with a full account of the trial of Mowbray and Henderson;[6] the judge's summing up of the case was amusing and instructive, as showing a sort of survival of the old sort of bullying of the Castlereagh times mixed with a grotesque attempt

---

of the preceding fortnight:

> It will be a cold day for those who prey upon our vitals if we ever serve them as they serve us… we can assure the humbugs and parasites of this neighbourhood that their dominion of cant will be strenuously attacked, and will be in danger of being destroyed.

5   The Merton Abbey Branch met at a working men's club at 11 Merton Terrace, High Street; customarily such clubs were licensed to sell alcoholic beverages only to members.

6   Probably Morris obtained the Norwich Saturday papers on Monday 24 January; both *The Norfolk News* and *Eastern Evening News* for that day record the judge's speech in great detail (*NN* p. 4 col. 1; *EEN* p. 4 cols. 2-3); the *Eastern Evening News'* summary is about 2,000 words. The Judge's self-righteous tone explains Morris's reference to a modernised Castlereagh:

Merton Abbey (Courtesy of the William Morris Gallery)

Photograph of Fred Henderson (*The Labour Prophet,* December 1892)

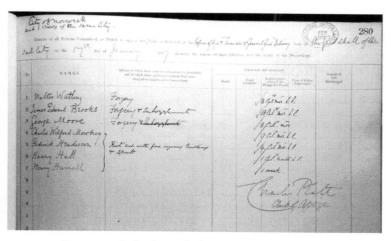

Court records for the trial of Mowbray and Henderson

at modernisation on philanthropical lines: it put me in a great rage.[7] The *Daily News*[8] printed my letter;[9] it had also a brief paragraph asserting that, Germany would presently ask France the meaning of her war-preparations, and an alarmist article therewith.[10] I did not know but what the other papers had the same news, and was much excited at the idea: because whatever one may say, one cannot help hoping that such a huge turmoil as a European war could not fail to turn to some advantage for us.[11] Coming to town however I found that the evening papers pooh pooh it as a mere hurrying up of the belated *Daily News*.[12] Yet there may be something in it.

        ... there was no town where the working class were more cared for... than Norwich... He was happy to know that in this country there was no reason why anyone should starve... In most large towns there were always a certain numbers of loafers who would rather be idling on a very small pittance than be flourishing on handiwork... Now he hoped that the working men of Norwich would take warning from that which had happened.

[7]   Morris included a rather vitriolic note on Justice Grantham in the 'Notes on Passing Events' for the 29 January *Commonweal.*

[8]   With a circulation of 150,000 by 1870, the *Daily News* was London's chief Liberal newspaper and provided more information on London events than *The Times*. It was Morris's favourite newspaper. Its emotional, editorialising tone brought out responsive traits in his temperament, and he engaged in a daily struggle with its contents. Although of course he disapproved of its hostility to Socialism, he tended to accept its interpretation of predictions of parliamentary and foreign events.

[9]   Morris's letter, dated 22 January, appeared in the *Daily News* of 24 January under the title, 'Disturbances at Norwich', following an article, 'The Socialists and Unemployed' and preceding notices on the 'Trial of Socialists' (in Berlin) and 'Socialist Disturbances in Belgium'.

[10] The brief paragraph stating that Germany will ask France the meaning of war preparations appeared on p. 5 col.3, under the title, 'Germany and France/War Impending', and the alarmist article is the p. 4 editorial, cols.7-8, 'Peace or War'.

[11] This is characteristic of a general apocalyptic optimism in Morris's interpretation of contemporary events during this relatively early period of his socialism. In his hope that a general European conflict would aid the socialists, he resembled Peter Kropotkin, with whom he shared many speaking platforms and conversations.

[12] *The Standard*, a conservative morning paper, was already angry at its more successful competitor on 24 January; although it did not cite the *Daily News* by name, on p. 5 col.5 its European correspondent sermonised:

At the Council of the Socialist League in the evening:[13] the Avelings[*] there mighty civil, but took no part in the proceedings.[14]

> The responsibility for the war scare which has prevailed for the last two days... rests, according to the leading Vienna paper, with the English Press alone. It is to the London papers, we are told, which are incessantly inciting France and Germany against each other... that the panic and depression on the Exchange are due.

By contrast, the chief evening paper, the *Pall Mall Gazette*, was reasonably laconic. Under the headline, 'Is War Impending Between France and Germany', p. 6, it cited the *Daily News*' comments, and added in its news summaries on the same page, 'At Home and Abroad', the noncommittal statement: 'The *Daily News* gives prominence to a startling rumour that there is imminent risk of almost immediate war between France and Germany'.

[13] At the time the Council consisted of Edward Aveling, H.A. Barker, E.B. Bax, Reg. A. Beckett, Thomas Binning, Henry Charles, A.K. Donald, W. Knight, Joseph Lane, Sam Mainwaring, Charles Mowbray, H.H. Sparling, Lena Wardle, Thomas Wardle, and Philip Webb.

[*] Aveling had been on a lecturing tour of some four months in America. (Morris's note)

Eleanor Marx Aveling (Source: Wiki)

Charles Bradlaugh 1890 (Courtesy of the National Portrait Gallery)

A dullish meeting, both sides rather shy of the Norwich matter, which but for the heaviness of the sentences would be but a pitiful affair: a committee was appointed to see after Mowbray's wife and children while he is *in*:[15] a letter came from Norwich with the news of their

---

[14] As leaders of the League's parliamentary faction, the Avelings were Morris's chief opponents in League affairs. He may have disliked them; in a letter probably written in 1887 (Houghton Autograph file, dated 16 June, to 'my dear Charles', [Henry F. Charles], Kelvin 2:668-69), he noted that even if the rival group took control, it would 'be burdened by the luckless Aveling & Mrs Eleanor who are not treasures for any association'. In January 1887 Aveling was 'luckless' since in their American tour of September-December 1886, he had created more than $2,000 of debts for the American SDF, and the London *Daily Telegraph* of 1 January and *Evening Standard* of 13 January had reported the news at home. In January the Avelings gave lectures comparing the conditions of the British and American working classes; e. g., *Commonweal* records one by each given 26 January. (29 January, p. 38; 5 February, p 47)

[15] Throughout the period of the *Diary*, the committee of Joseph Lane, Henry Charles, and H. A. Barker reported contributions in *Commonweal*; by 5 March they had collected £25. Contributions by Morris of £1 each were recorded in the issues of 12 and 19 February.

having held a great meeting of 6000 in the market place on Sunday at which they passed resolutions condemning the sentence, and in favour of the Social Revolution: though I fear few indeed out of the 6000 knew what that meant. They were getting up a petition to the Home Secretary.[16]

Our attempt to get up an Irish meeting of the Radicals led by the Socialists will fail: we are not big enough for the job: the Radical Clubs are civil to us but afraid of us and not yet prepared to break with the Liberals. Donald proposed to accept the challenge thrown out by Bradlaugh to the Socialists to debate with him;[17] Donald's proposal included a paper debate of six articles, three on each side, to be carried on in the *Commonweal*, or Bradlaugh in *C[ommonweal]*, and our champion in the *National Reformer*. The whole meeting in spirits at the idea: but surely Bradlaugh is too old a cat to drag that straw.[18] More by token Andreas Scheu was chosen as the oral debater and Bax as the

---

[16] Probably a false report, since neither the Norwich papers, the London papers, nor *Commonweal* mention such a large meeting or a petition on the matter. The 29 January *Commonweal* reports no information from the Norwich Branch, and the report for 5 February merely mentions that five 'well attended' meetings were held throughout the city the preceding Sunday (30 January, which would have been after Morris's entry), then adds the assertion: 'We are not daunted because our comrades Mowbray and Henderson are in Norwich Castle, but intend to work on all the more'. Surely a successful mass protest meeting would have inspired comment.

[17] Earlier in the month, Charles Bradlaugh had begun a lecture series at the Hall of Science entitled 'Socialism, its Fallacies and Dangers'. Morris is referring to Bradlaugh's statement on the first page of the *National Reformer* of 23 January:

Complaints have been made that there is not sufficient opportunity for discussion at the Hall of Science Sunday morning lectures of the objections stated by me against socialism. I am willing, if it is desired, to meet in formal debate — and on similar conditions to those in the Hyndman discussion — any representative selected by the Socialist Democratic Federation or the Socialist League. Two gentlemen have already intimated their desire to discuss. I must at present wait until some representative selection is made by the Federation or League, and until the question proposed for debate is reduced to writing.

[18] Possibly in the sense of 'to smoke a pipe', as in *OED* meaning II.10.d. for 'straw': 'a slender kind of clay pipe'; the example cited is dated 1882.

Troy Tapestry 1887 (Courtesy of the Victoria and Albert Museum)

literary:[19] Everyone relished the idea of seeing Scheu and Bradlaugh face to face; both of them so combative and dogmatic: that with the addition that Scheu would be sure to get the best of C[harles] B[radlaugh] quite put us in spirits: but of course Bradlaugh will find some way of escape.[20]

This morning the *Daily News* still sticks to its guns; but I am inclined to think it was a canard bred out of the great probability of the thing.

26 Jan[uary]: Went to S[outh] K[ensington] M[useum][21] yesterday with Jenny to look at the Troy tapestry again since they have bought it for £1250:[22] I chuckled to think that properly speaking it was bought for

---

[19] At the time Ernest Belfort Bax would have had an additional motive for debating with Bradlaugh: see the unfriendly review of Bax's *The Religion of Socialism* in the *National Reformer*, 16 January 1887.

[20] Morris was in this case too suspicious; the Bax-Bradlaugh debate was published in *Commonweal* later in the year, from 21 May–28 July. The oral debate never occurred. The Amsterdam IISH Scheu collection contains H.A. Barker's letter of 26 January inviting Scheu to participate in the debate, Scheu's refusal of 27 January, a renewed SL Council invitation signed by Donald, Binning, Barker, and Wardle, and Scheu's reiterated refusal on 4 February on the grounds that he had already accepted a speaking engagement for that date.

[21] For many years Morris had maintained close ties with the South Kensington (now Victoria and Albert) Museum (SKM). In 1886 the museum's founder, Henry Cole, commissioned one of the firm's first important orders, for its Green Dining Room. Morris visited the museum repeatedly to gain ideas for his designs, and the dates of some of these can be correlated with specific museum acquisitions. During this period Morris served as the SKM's chief advisor for the purchase of tapestries, several of which were acquired on his recommendation.

[22] Morris had argued for the purchase of the Flemish 'Tapestry of the Siege of Troy' (now in Victoria and Albert (V & A) Gallery 38, 6-1887), woven during what he considered the best period of medieval tapestry weaving, the early fifteenth century. The 'Siege of Troy' was received by the SKM on 13 November 1886, and catalogued in early January. Since his early 20s, Morris's identification with heroic defeats in love and war had attracted him to the Troy legend; it appears in references in 'Sir Peter Harpdon's End' in *The Defence of Guenevere* and his dramatic fragment of the 1860s, 'Scenes from the Fall of Troy'. Morris's interest in tapestry was reflected again in the same year by the firm's completion of 'The Forest', now in the V & A Museum.

me, since scarcely anybody will care a damn for it. A. Cole showed us a lot of scraps of woven stuff from the tombs of Upper Egypt; very curious as showing in an unusual material the transition to the pure Byzantine style from the Classical:[23] some pieces being nothing but debased Classical style, others purely Byzantine, yet I think not much different in date: the contrast between the bald ugliness of the Classical pieces and the great beauty of the Byzantine was a pleasing thing to me, who loathe so all Classical art and literature.[24] I spoke in the evening at the Hammersmith radical club[25] at a meeting to condemn the Glenbeigh evictions. The room crowded, and of course our Socialist friends there, my speech was well received, but I thought the applause rather hollow as the really radical part of the audience had clearly no ideas beyond the ordinary party shibboleths, and were quite untouched by Socialism: they seemed to me a very discouraging set of men; but perhaps can be got at somehow. The frightful ignorance and want of impressibility of the average English workman floors me at times.

---

[23] The museum acquired a large number of Egyptian textiles from 1886–88, now in Room 100, Case F, 'Late Antique and Early Medieval Textiles'. The classical textiles which Morris disliked may be the contents of approx. drawers 1–29, from the third and fourth centuries; in the fifth- or sixth-century weaving of drawer 46, with its rose, pink, orange, yellow, dark blue, blue green, and purple threads, one can find a striking confirmation of the change he describes. For a description of these collections, see Alan S. Cole, *A Supplementary Descriptive Catalogue of Tapestry-Wove and Embroidered Egyptian Textiles. Acquired for the South Kensington Museum between 1886 and June 1890*, London 1891.

[24] Morris frequently deprecated classical literature in general terms, but these comments from the author of *The Life and Death of Jason*, twelve classical *Earthly Paradise* tales, and translations of Homer and Virgil should not be taken too literally; within the week he was working on his 'Odyssey' at Rottingdean; see entry for 3 February. In an 1885 list of his fifty-four favourite books solicited by the editor of the *Pall Mall Gazette*, he includes three Latin and six Greek titles, and adds grudgingly, 'Of course I admit the archaeological value of some of them, especially Virgil and Ovid'. His comments on the 'classical' should be read as a defense of romantic values in art and rejection of the nineteenth-century academic preference for ancient and classical over medieval European culture.

[25] On King Street. The 1882–87 Glenbeigh evictions on the estate of Lord Wynne in County Kerry, Ireland were conducted with unusual ferocity; in some cases cottagers' homes and possessions were torched.

27 [January]. I went to Merton yesterday on a lovely day: Wardle[26] told me the whole story of what they are doing and are going to do at St. Mark's at Venice.[27] I was incoherent with rage: they will soon finish up the whole thing there — and indeed everywhere else. I suppose the 'anti-scrape' will make one last stand for it;[28] but a few archeologists, and archeological Socialists cannot resist civilization (be damned to it!): nor are the 'Italians' (the bourgeoisie of course) much worse than other people; though I think as to matters of history [plus?] art, they must divide the prize with the Germans: both French and English being a trifle better.[29]

---

[26] George Wardle had been commissioned by the Society for the Protection of Ancient Buildings (see footnote 28) to visit Venice to investigate the restorations at St Mark's (see footnote 27). A report, signed by him and Professor Middleton and dated 24 May 1887, appeared in the 1888 SPAB *Annual Report*, pp. 61-69.

[27] Ruskin's *Stones of Venice*, 1851–53, had made St Mark's Cathedral one of the buildings most admired by British artists and intellectuals. At a protest meeting held in the Sheldonian Theatre in November 1879, George Street, the prominent architect for whom Morris had once worked, proposed a resolution against any alterations, describing St Mark's as 'the most exquisite piece of colour and architecture in Europe', and Morris gave a supporting speech. Despite an extended campaign to persuade the Italian government to curtail restoration, the government did 'finish up the whole thing there'.

[28] In 1877 Morris and others founded 'anti-scrape', The Society for the Protection of Ancient Buildings, still in existence; a copy of G.F. Watts' portrait of Morris painted by Henry Holiday hangs in the central room of its current headquarters in 37 Spital Square, EC1. At the time, Morris still served as one of its honorary secretaries, and the *Diary* may underplay the organising work which this required during the period.

[29] 1886 and 1887 SPAB annual reports indicate that the two recently founded French branches of the Society were its most active continental allies. The report's hopeful assessments of more widespread continental interest — 'the zeal which is now beginning to be exhibited for the preservation of national antiquities, particularly in France and Germany' (1887 Annual Report) — contrast sharply with Morris's private exasperation. For discussions of the SPAB's continental campaigns, see Frank C. Sharp, 'A Lesson in International Relations: Morris and the SPAB,' *JWMS* 10.2 (Spring 1993): 9-15 and Andrea Donovan, *William Morris and the Society for the Protection of Ancient Buildings*, Routledge, 2007.

Parliament is to meet today: that is not of much importance to 'we-uns'.[30] It is a matter of course that if the Government venture to bring forward a gagging-bill they will not venture to make it anything but an Irish one.[31] For my part I should rather like the Liberals to get in again:[32] for if they do, they must either push on the revolution by furthering Irish matters, which will be a direct gain to us; or they must sneak out of the Irish question which would be an indirect gain to us, but a far greater one, as it would turn all that is democratic sick of them. It seems that they by no means want to get in, and I don't wonder, considering that dilemma.

News this morning that Goschen has lost Liverpool;[33] the *Daily News* of course in high spirits;[34] and since Goschen won't like it of course I do. Probably it will somewhat damage the Tories, and also serve as a show

---

[30] In the previous July elections, Gladstonian Liberals suffered heavy defeat; the Conservatives won 316 seats, the Liberals 276, and 78 'Liberal Unionists', Liberals who had voted against their party on Home Rule, gave the Conservatives a strong majority of 394. Although long since disaffected with Gladstonian liberalism, Morris's *Commonweal* notes indicate that he enjoyed disagreeing with his former party.

[31] As laws restricting free speech, 'gagging bills' were of crucial importance to the socialists. The Conservatives' Irish Coercion bill was passed as the Crimes Act of July 1887.

[32] Since the Liberals had long been the dominant party and expected to continue to be so under the widened franchise, they still hoped for a return to power. As the leader of the anti-Home Rule Liberals, Joseph Chamberlain made two abortive efforts at conciliation with Gladstone in the early months of 1887, but when the second of these failed in April, the rift widened. Except for a three-year period 1892–95, the Conservatives were to continue in power until nine years after Morris's death.

[33] The Conservatives had appointed as Chancellor of the Exchequer the Liberal Unionist George Goschen. Goschen had insisted on the removal of Lord Iddesleigh from the foreign office, and when the old man died suddenly after taking leave of his staff, Goschen lost popularity and was defeated by eleven votes in a by-election at Liverpool. Although the government was embarrassed, he was soon re-elected from the Conservative stronghold of St George's, Hanover Square, which remained his constituency for the next thirteen years. Morris particularly disliked Goschen; in the week's *Commonweal* (29 January) he described a Goschen campaign speech as 'remarkable for emptiness, dullness, and twaddle'.

[34] The *Daily News* did all it could to aggrandise the victory of the Liberal candidate Neville by eleven of 6,433 votes cast. By the 'equal balance of the electorate,' Morris of course refers to the slender margin of victory.

to Chamberlain to make some sort of terms with the Gladstonites: it all looks very like a compromise and the Liberals coming in. It is curious to see how equally the parties are balanced in the electorate, by the way: and this again is hopeful for us, because it will force the Liberals to be less and less democratic, and so consolidate the Party of Reaction.[35]

Feb[ruary]3rd. Went down to Rottingdean[36] on Friday 28th and spent three or four days there: was very glad to leave the Newspapers alone while there: did Homer[37] and an article for *Commonweal*, which last was weak, long and no use:[38] got a surprise on Monday by hearing that Janey and Jenny are going to Rome with the Howards.[39] I was very loth to

---

[35] Even Morris may have felt this optimism a bit strained; note the next sentence's relief at his temporary suspension of newspaper commentary.

[36] In 1881 Morris's closest friend Edward Burne-Jones and his family had bought the small 'North End House' near the sea at Rottingdean, four miles east of Brighton.

[37] Morris's translation of the *Odyssey*, published in April and November 1887, is described by Geoffrey Riddehough in 'William Morris's Translation of the *Odyssey*', *Journal of English and Germanic Philology*, vol. 40 (1941), pp. 558-61. Riddehough criticises Morris's use of saga mannerisms and other archaisms, but notes that 'actual blunders are remarkably few, if we consider the translation as the hurried spare-time work of an unusually busy man,' and respects 'an odd tendency to bring out the ancient meaning of a word...'.

[38] It is possible but unlikely that Morris is referring to the fourteenth chapter of his joint work with Bax, *The Roots of Socialism*, which appeared as 'The Transition from the Utopists to Modern Socialism' in the *Commonweal* of 5 February; the uneven and pedantic style of the chapter suggests Bax rather than Morris. More probably Morris alludes to an early draft for an article which appeared 19 February, 'Facing the Worst of It', in which Morris wrote of socialists' response to immediate frustration that: 'it is well for us not to be too sanguine, since overwhelming hope is apt to give birth to despair if it meets with check or disappointment.'

[39] Morris may be intentionally laconic here. Jane Morris's trips abroad for health and companionship were expensive; in the 1870s they had been a serious financial burden, although by now he could afford them more easily. Moreover his family's absence may have left him somewhat lonely; Morris's letters indicate that he missed his daughter Jenny during her absences. Jenny was twenty-six and had suffered for nine years from seizures which signaled a progressively deteriorative muscular and brain disease; the Morrises hoped the trip would benefit Jenny's as well as Jane's health. Twenty-five-year-old May remained with her father, and *Commonweal* records her frequent

come back; though as for Holidays, 'tis a mistake to call them rests: one is excited and eager always; at any rate during a short holiday, and I don't know what a long one means. The ordinary drifting about of a 'busy' man is much less exciting than these sort of holidays.

They have got at their parliamentary twaddle fairly by this time.[40] Everybody all agog about Randolph Churchill's speech and his hard hits at the Liberal Unionist allies of the Tories:[41] the whole debate duller even than usual, and quite beneath notice of any kind. The day before yesterday the *Standard* had a very alarmist article on the war-scare: I suppose it really is coming.[42] That evening I took the chair at a debate between Annie Besant and Foote:[43] she was fairly good, though too

---

activities for the SL; she served as a League librarian and contributed occasional literary notices and French and Italian news summaries to *Commonweal*. Letters preserved at the IISH indicate that she also helped her father with SL correspondence.

[40] Despite disclaimers, recent political events had frustrated him; see his outburst in the *Cw*'s introductory 'Notes on News' for 5 February, responding to Chamberlain's appeal to constituencies to show gratitude for past services:

> Gratitude to traitors and turncoats! Sham sentiment of the nineteenth century, you do indeed get into curious corners when politicians deal with you!… the rule now is that when a man has got a reputation as a leader he may indulge himself in almost any shabbiness and sneaking ways… always so long as he brazens it out, and keeps himself well before the public — advertises himself, in fact.

[41] Since Randolph Churchill had just resigned as Chancellor of the Exchequer (his replacement by Goschen had led to the Liverpool by-election) and House leader of the Conservative party, his lengthy, irritable, and mocking speech of 31 January (reprinted in *The Times*, 1 February, pp. 6-7) elicited interest; he attacked his party for relying on a possibly fickle alliance with the Liberal Unionists and their House of Lords leader, Lord Hartington. Threatening them with future loss of power, he exhorted them instead to rely on 'good government' and insulted their new allies: 'I frankly admit that I regarded the Liberal Unionists as a useful kind of crutch.'

[42] In contrast to its disapproval of a similar reaction the previous week by the *Daily News*, on 31 January the *Standard*'s article 'The Peace of Europe' (p. 5 cols. 5-6) asserted, 'The European situation is still regarded as most critical, there being a general apprehension that war between Germany and France within a very short time is almost certain.'

[43] This was a four-week debate, 2, 9, 16 and 23 February, between Annie Besant and George Foote at the Hall of Science, 142 Old Street, City Road, EC, on the question, 'Is Socialism Sound?' Morris chaired the first session, Shaw the

Rosalind Howard c. 1860 (Courtesy of the William Morris Gallery)

Annie Besant 1891 (Courtesy of the National Portrait Gallery)

George William Foote (Courtesy of Conway Hall, London)

Bradlaughian in manner; she has advanced somewhat in her Socialism.[44] Foote was nothing special; the ordinary well-practiced secularist speaker. It seems he is a land-nationalizer, which I didn't know.[45] The audience (naturally, as it was in the Secularists' own ground) was about two-thirds anti-socialist.

Feb[ruary] 7th (Monday). On Friday I went up to the Chiswick Club, where Mordhurst (one of our Hammersmith Branch) was to have opened a debate on the class-war, but as he didn't turn up, I was called on to take his place:[46] the room was not large; about twenty people there

---

third, and revised texts of both debates were later published as *Is Socialism Sound: A Verbatim Report... Revised by both disputants*, Progressive Publishing Co., London 1887, along with the introductory remarks; Morris introduced the debate as on '*the* question of the day'.

44 In 1886, Annie Besant left her ten-year association with Bradlaugh in order to campaign for a mild version of socialism. Her speech advocates 'scientific socialism', which she defines in contrast to 'utopian socialism' as a change in the economic order of society. Although her rhetoric is vague: 'I submit that Socialism is no longer a dream. It is a reasoned scheme based on political economy. It proposes to change our economic basis. It proposes to do this by rational and thoughtful argument, convincing the brain of man,' the shift Morris refers to may be shown in her belief that under socialism no private property in materials will be necessary for the production of wealth. (*Is Socialism Sound?*, p. 5)

45 Actually, it's hard to tell from his remarks that evening whether Foote advocated land nationalisation. Although he comments towards the end of his second address of the evening that 'Mrs Besant is a land nationaliser as well as I' (*Is Socialism Sound?*, p. 28), he argued rather deviously that Herbert Spencer has claimed the right of all to access of nature, so land nationalisation is not a socialist idea. (pp. 16-17) Moreover, the state could rent land at unequal rates for different qualities of land, and so capitalistic risk and profit-taking would still be possible and even inevitable. He goes on to stress the need for unequal wealth on Malthusian principles, and as a reward for unequal talents. The effect of his remarks is to reduce 'land nationalisation' to a virtual re-description of the status quo. In general Foote uses declamatory generalisation and sarcasm to reduce his opponents' arguments to tautology or absurdity, and avoids debate on the desirability of socialism.

46 Although the Hammersmith Socialist Society Minutes (BL Add. MSS 45,891-93) indicate advance planning, the Chiswick Club debate hadn't been announced in the previous week's *Commonweal*, an unusual omission. C. Henry Mordhurst was one of the branch's steady propagandists in this period.

at first; swelling to forty perhaps before the end: the kind of men composing the audience is a matter worth noting, since the chief purpose of this diary is to record my impressions on the Socialist movement. I should say then that the speakers were all either of the better-to-do workmen or small tradesmen class: except Gordon Hogg who is a doctor and is trying to push himself forward so as to get himself into parliament on the democratic side; he seems more than half a Socialist. My Socialism was gravely listened to by the audience but taken with no enthusiasm; and in fact however simply one puts the case for Socialism one always rather puzzles an audience: the speakers, except Hogg and a young timid member of our branch, were muddled to the last degree; but clearly the most intelligent men did not speak: the debate was adjourned till next Friday, but I was allowed a short reply in which I warmed them up somehow: this description of an audience may be taken for almost any other at a Radical Club, *mutatis mutandis*. The sum of it all is that the men at present listen respectfully to Socialism, but are perfectly supine and not in the least inclined to move except along the lines of radicalism and trades Unionism. I ought to have noted that, on the day that Parliament met, a young and new M.P., Cunninghame Graham by name, called on me by appointment to pump me on the subject of Socialism, and we had an agreeable talk. A brisk bright sort of young man; the other day he made his maiden speech and produced quite an impression by its brilliancy and socialistic hints.[47] His opinion of Chamberlain by the way is that of others who are engaged in party politics, to wit that he is a self-seeker pure and simple and that he set on foot this Unionist business out of sheer spite against Gladstone.

Yesterday Sunday we began our open-air meetings at Beadon R[oa]d:[48] near the Broadway there. I spoke alone for about an hour, and

---

[47] In his identification with the oppressed, R.B. Cunninghame-Graham was unique in the parliament of the day.

[48] Outdoor Hammersmith Branch SL station, northwest of the Hammersmith underground station; see map of Hammersmith in 1887. Since Beadon Road doesn't appear on London ordinance maps for 1878, it may have been built shortly before; London survey records indicate that it was named in 1880. The Hammersmith Branch changed the location of its outdoor stations several times in an effort to maintain an audience; the Hammersmith Socialist Society Minutes record earlier attempts on King Street by Weltje Road and at the south of Hammersmith Bridge, and the selection on 4 April 1886 of a site in Beadon Road at the back of the Liberal Club.

a very fair audience (for the place which is out of the [way]) gathered curiously quickly; a comrade counted a hundred at most. This audience characteristic of small open air meetings also quite mixed, from labourers on their Sunday lounge to 'respectable' people coming from church: the latter inclined to grin: the working men listening attentively trying to understand, but mostly failing to do so: a fair cheer when I ended, of course led by the three or four branch members present. The meeting in the evening poor. Hyndman at the Chiswick Club.[49] I saw Janey and Jenny off to Rome on Saturday:[50] news this morning of their happy arrival at Paris.

Feb[ruary] 12th. I have been on League business every night this week till tonight. Monday the Council meeting:[51] peaceable enough and dull: G.B. Shaw was proposed and accepted as our champion against Bradlaugh;[52] there was talk of the Norwich defence fund and the

---

[49] Hyndman's talk is not mentioned in *Commonweal*. The 5 February *Justice* announced that on the 6th at 8 p.m. he would speak at the Chiswick Club on 'The Causes of Social Revolution', although for some reason the 12 February *Justice* omitted a report on the event.

[50] Morris's letters to his daughter and wife during their absence are preserved in BL Add. MS. 45,339 (Jenny, Kelvin 2:613-48 passim) and BL Add. MS. 45,338 (Jane, Kelvin 2:644). They seem to have returned on 16 May, for in a letter to Joseph Lane of that date Morris states that his wife and Jenny are returning home that evening (British Library 46,345, Kelvin 2:650), and Morris mentions their recent arrival in a letter to his mother dated 24 May (William Morris Gallery, Kelvin 2:659). On 3 June Jane Morris wrote to Rosalind Howard that 'there is no doubt that Jenny has benefited in every way, her father is delighted with the change in her, she is more like her old self than she has ever been since her illness began 11 years ago' (Autograph letter, Howard Castle Archive, Sharp and Marsh, *Letters JM*, 153).

[51] Council meetings were held at the League's offices at 13 Farringdon Road, EC1.

[52] G.B. Shaw's correspondence with the League secretary Henry A. Barker appears in his *Collected Letters: 1874–1897*, London 1965, pp. 164-66. Shaw seems to have felt concern over his role in the proposed contest:

> Therefore, though for personal reasons I am anxious to avoid any course that may strain the friendly relations which Mr Bradlaugh's services to the people have established between him and my colleagues as well as myself, I cannot refuse to accept… Only let it be understood that I am not the challenger and that I did not volunteer for the defence. (9 February, pp. 164-5)

Commune Celebration:[53] also election of three new members to Council, all workmen.[54] Tuesday I took the chair at the meeting to protest against the (possible) coming war at Cleveland Hall, Cleveland S[tree]t:[55] a wretched place once flash and now sordid in a miserable street.[56] It is the head-quarters of what I should call the orthodox Anarchists: Victor Dave the leading spirit there. Of course there were many 'foreigners' there, and also a good sprinkling of our people and I suppose of the Federation also. It was rather hard work getting through all the speeches in the unknown tongues of French and German, and the natives showed their almost superstitious reverence for

---

[53] The celebration of the anniversary of the Paris Commune was an important annual socialist event, held in 1887 on 17 March at South Place Chapel. In his *Commonweal* article of 19 March, 'Why we Celebrate the Commune of Paris', Morris expressed his characteristic emphasis on extracting achievement from failure:

> I have heard it said, and by good Socialists too, that it is a mistake to commemorate a defeat… The Commune of Paris is but one link in the struggle which has gone through all the history of the oppressed against the oppressors; and without all the defeats of past times we should now have no hope of the final victory.

[54] Members of the Council elected for the first time in 1887 were James Allman, W. Blundell, C. Burcham, S. Cantwell, H.B. Tarleton, J.J. Graham, and A. Davis. Of these Allman was a tailor's presser from the Mile End branch, Tarleton was from the Hammersmith branch, and the remaining four were from North London.

[55] The *Commonweal* of 5 February had announced that:

> A meeting of the international revolutionists to protest against the Coming War will be held in Cleveland Hall, Cleveland Street, Portland Road, W., on Tuesday February 8, at 8 p.m. The chair will be taken by comrade Morris. Speeches will be made in various languages…

and the 12 February issue printed a friendly report, noting that 'speeches were made in several languages by men of the different peoples' and that 'a strong resolution was unanimously carried'.

[56] According to *Commonweal*, this was 54 Cleveland Street near Portland Road Station (now Great Portland Street Station); north of Soho, it was in an area with a large immigrant population, and the SL branch contained several exiles, including Victor Dave (Belgian), Henry Charles (German), and (before his departure to Edinburgh) Andreas Scheu (Austrian). It was strongly anti-parliamentarian, and by 'orthodox anarchists' Morris refers to the fact that they had not joined the successionist Autonomy Group (see footnotes 57 and 58).

internationalism by sitting through it all patiently: the foreign speakers were mostly of the 'orthodox Anarchists'; but a collectivist also spoke, and one at least of the Autonomy section[57] who have some quarrel which I can't understand with the Cleveland Hall people:[58] a Federation man spoke though he was not a delegate; also Macdonald of the Socialist Union:[59] the Fabians declined to send on the grounds of the war-scare being premature; but probably in reality because they did not want to be mixed up too much with the Anarchists:[60] the Kropotkin-Wilson people[61] also refused on the grounds that Bourgeois peace is a war,[62]

---

[57] A dispute between Victor Dave and a fellow member of the Whitfield Street Club of leftist exiles, a younger Austrian anarcho-communist Josef Peukert, led the latter and his associates in 1886 to form a separate Gruppe Autonomie (Autonomy Group), which met at 32 Charlotte Street, Fitzroy Square (and later at 6 Windmill Street, Tottenham Court Road) and published *Die Autonomie* from 6 November 1886 until 22 April 1893. For an account of their personal and ideological differences and the resultant 'Bruderkrieg', see Andrew Carlson, *Anarchism in Germany*, Metuchen, N.J., Scarecrow, 1972, chap. 10. Carlson sees Dave as maintaining an older, Bakuninist, authoritarian anarchism and Peukert as advocating a less hierarchical anarcho-communism, which emphasised voluntarism and mutual aid.

[58] Hostilities had intensified when the Autonomy Group accepted the credentials of Karl Theodor Reuss, whom the Cleveland Hall people believed was a spy, and whom the SL voted to expel on 10 May 1886. The Cleveland Hall group were right, and Reuss's testimony eventually led to the imprisonment and death of an important and devoted European anarchist, Johann Neve; this in turn gave rise to a painful series of charges and counentercharges. Neve had been arrested on 21 February 1887, and Reuss confessed his guilt in October of the same year. Carlson's *Anarchism in Germany* (chap. II, 'John Neve and the Split in the Movement') skilfully unravels the complex and tragic deceptions, uncertainties, and conflicts which followed on this event. Anarchist factionalism has been frequently derided, but much of the information the anarchists needed for self-protection was unavailable to them, and was only recoverable decades later from police files.

[59] After the departure of SDF members to form the SL in 1885, another defection from the SDF, this time of committed parliamentarians, occurred in 1886, when Hyndman's use of Conservative Party campaign money ('Tory Gold') became known. The seceding group called itself the Socialist Union and published a paper, *The Socialist*, but had disbanded by early 1887. James Macdonald, a prominent member, then returned to the SDF (Chushichi Tsuzuki, *H. M. Hyndman and British Socialism*, Oxford 1961, p. 72); also see Macdonald's remarks in a *Justice* interview, 11 July 1896, p. 6.

which no doubt was a genuine reason on their part and is true enough: but of course the meeting was meant to be a protest against the Bourgeois whether in peace or war, and also to keep alive the idea of a

---

[60] Since in the 1880s almost every group which strongly disliked the current government defined itself as 'socialist', it was inevitable that real political oppositions would appear between the Fabians, who were evolving into advocates of a strong state-planned centralised economy, and the anarchists, who advocated decentralisation, various degrees of mutualism, and the withering away of institutionalised government. For example, note the Fabian G.B. Shaw's letter to Henry Barker of the same month in which he binds himself to maintain against Bradlaugh only:

> That it is advisable to abandon the principle of individualism for that of socialism; and that this change of policy can be made effective only by complete resumption of the land, with a transfer of the existing capital of the country from its present holders to the state.

It is 'individualism', not class-antagonism, oppression of workers, or denial of self-determination that is the central focus of his attack. (Shaw, *Collected Letters*, p. 166)

[61] In October 1886 Peter Kropotkin and Charlotte Wilson had begun an anarchist journal, *Freedom: A Journal of Anarchist Socialism*, and its supporters were called the Freedom Group, with headquarters at 34 Bouverie Street, EC4. Quail (p. 57) states that although anti-parliamentarian, it shared with the Fabians an exclusiveness, middle-class constituency, and desire to permeate and organise other groups. *Freedom* was printed at the *Commonweal* press (27 Farringdon Road, EC), and was distributed along with their own publications at SL branch meetings; the Freedom Group maintained some membership in common with the SL. (Quail, p. 59) The SL anarchist David Nicholl wrote in *Commonweal* sixteen years later that:

> ... neither Kitz, Mowbray, or I were particularly friendly [to the Freedom Group]. We looked upon them as a collection of middle class faddists, who took up with the movement as an amusement, and regretted that Kropotkin and other 'serious' people ever had anything to do with them. (3 October 1903, Quail, p. 59)

[62] In early 1887 Kropotkin apparently believed in the inevitability of immediate war (Woodcock and Avakomovic, *The Anarchist Prince*, London 1950, p. 225), and he seems also to have been hopeful that such a war might further a revolutionary uprising. His general position, as expressed for example in *Memoirs of a Revolutionist*, London, Swan Sonnenschein, 1906, pp. 167, 252, 270-72, and 466-67), did not diverge greatly from views Morris advanced here in the diary, in the *Commonweal* article quoted in note 63 below, and in other expressions of his views on social revolution.

revolt behind the Bourgeois and Absolutist armies if the war did happen.[63] This same Tuesday the SDF had announced a meeting on Clerkenwell Green and a torch-light procession westward in commemoration of last year's riot:[64] a stupid thing to do unless they really had strength and resolution to make a big row, which they *know* they have not got. Of course Sir C[harles] Warren proclaimed the procession;[65] so the leaders drew back but the rank and file determined

---

[63] Morris viewed war as destructive of foreign and British working-class interests, and during his lifetime never advocated British involvement in a war. Early in his political career he wrote in an 1877 placard on the Turkish question (JI43, WMorris Gal, Henderson, *Letters*, pp. 388-89) addressed 'To the workingmen of England':

> There is danger of war; bestir yourselves to face that danger... for a hard matter it will be for most of us to bear war-taxes, war-prices, war-losses of wealth and work, and friends and kindred: we shall pay heavily, and you, friends of the working classes, will pay the heaviest.

In *News from Nowhere* the advent of socialism is accompanied by limited civil war, but there is no massive European struggle. Morris's contempt for British imperialism and militarism is also apparent in *News from Nowhere*'s description of the anti-socialist government's general, 'who had won a certain sort of reputation in the disgraceful wars in which the country had been long engaged from time to time.' (*CW*, vol. XVII chap. 17, p. 114) In his response to a recent London Peace Conference, in 'Notes on News', *Commonweal*, 26 July 1890 (p. 235), Morris wrote that 'this violent war of modern times, and the preparation for it, is just as much a part of the present capitalist system as banking is, and can no more be dispensed with than that.' Even at peace, the European nation states would maintain standing armies. '*To keep down the People!...* Those only are really seeking *peace* who are seeking *equality* first'.

[64] On 8 February 1886, at a demonstration in Trafalgar Square, SDF speakers persuaded the crowd to move to Hyde Park, and en route members of the crowd smashed windows and looted. The incident intensified police surveillance at socialist meetings and led to the arrest of four SDF members, Hyndman, Champion, Burns, and Williams, for whom Morris and Bax offered bail. After a trial which the prisoners described as impartial (*Justice*, 17 April 1886), they were acquitted. Since the publicity surrounding the riots had stressed the possibility of revolution, the attempt to rerun the event would have created an expectation of escalated violence. The 5 February *Commonweal* discreetly avoided announcing the mass meeting, although once it had occurred, the 12 February issue expressed solidarity with those arrested. (p. 55)

to hold the meeting and the procession. But the meeting was as good as nothing; the police easily stopped the procession, and a very small bit of window-breaking was all that happened.

Of course the papers made the most of it next morning and on Thursday was an elaborate account in the *Daily News* of the seige of a butcher's shop,[65] an incident of which all the papers had an account more or less.[67] But on Friday comes a note in the papers from Warren contradicting the whole story, which contradiction, by the way, some of our people confirmed.*[68] This is too good a joke to miss especially as all the papers printed Warren's contradiction as small as they durst and did

---

[65] The use of 'proclaim' in this context seems to have been fairly recent; definition 2e. of the *OED* reads 'To place (a district, country, etc.) under legal restrictions by proclamation: spec. under the provisions of the various Peace Preservation (Ireland) Acts of 1881 and following years,' and the related meaning 2f. appears here, 'To denounce or prohibit by proclamation; to forbid publicly or openly.' The two examples of usage cited are from 1885 and 1887, both from the press. In its 12 February capsule summary of the meeting, p. 55, *Commonweal* still placed 'proclaimed' in quotation marks.

[66] Interestingly there were three *Daily News* accounts, the first the most accurate. On Wednesday 9 February, p. 6 col.4, an article 'The Socialist Meeting' declared that the meeting had disbanded quietly, and reported without comment a report by 'The Central News' of a butcher's firing on the crowd. The *Daily News'* second account appeared on 10 February, p. 3 col.3, under the title 'The Socialist Demonstration in Clerkenwell', and is inserted in the *Diary*, p. 12. Five long paragraphs describe the mob's theft of £25 of meat, Mr Geering the butcher's firing of a pistol, spirited conversation between himself and the 'rabble', and his final defence of his premises with revolvers and an antiquated dagger. The tone now patronises the loquacious but valiant British shopkeeper. Still a third account, from the 'Press Associate', follows directly below in smaller type; this describes the smashing of windows in the shop of Mr Veering the butcher (note the different spelling) and others, omits mention of the butcher's firing on the mob, and assesses the total damage from window smashing as under £100.

[67] Under the title 'The Disturbances at Clerkenwell' (p. 8 col. 3), *The Times* for 10 February repeated the *Daily News'* account of 9 February almost verbatim. No wonder Morris laughed. Although the 10 February *Standard* reported 'The Socialist Riots' (p. 3 col.6), it cited the arrest of a coal porter but did not mention any butcher shop theft.

[68] * The butcher's shop was shuttered when the mob went by: they didn't stop there and he fired off his pistols twenty minutes after they had passed on: so Sir Ch[arles] Warren says. (Morris's note)

not give one word of excuse:[69] nay the *Pall Mall* did not even chaff the *Daily News* on its blunder.

On Wednesday I went to lecture at a schoolroom in Peckham High S[tree]t for some goody-goody literary society or other:[70] it was pretty different from my Tuesday's experience: the people were Christians and began the meeting with prayer and finished with a blessing. However it is worth noting that a good part of the audience (not a large one about one hundred I should think, there being counterattractions in the neighbourhood) was quite enthusiastic, though I suspect the presence of some of our people or the SDF there: also I should not forget that they gave me thirty s[hillings] towards our printing fund.

Thursday I went to the Ways and Means Committee at the League:[71] found them cheerful there on the prospects of *Commonweal*: I didn't feel as cheerful as the others,[72] but hope it may go on.

Friday I went in the evening to finish the debate begun last week:[73] the room full Sparling made a good speech; I didn't: the meeting having got very conversational by that time.

---

[69] The *Daily News'* Friday 11 February retraction was a small paragraph on p. 5 col.4, entitled 'The Riot in Clerkenwell' and followed by a letter 'To the Editor of the Daily News', reporting that the author had been directed to transmit the statement:

> There is no foundation for the statement circulated that shops were pillaged on the night of the 8th inst. in Compton-street and Goswell-road, near Clerkenwell, or that meat was stolen from a butcher's shop in Compton-street... .

The 11 February *Daily Standard* also carried the retraction. (p. 3 col. 3, under the notice 'The Clerkenwell Riot ')

[70] Unidentified; Canon Ridley was chair; see LeMire Cal, p. 261 and Morris's engagement calendar on that date. (BL Add. MS. 45,408)

[71] The meeting of the Ways and Means Committee is absent from LeMire Cal; it was probably held at the League office, 13 Farringdon Road, EC1.

[72] Since Morris was paying, they could afford more cheerfulness. Later in the year he estimated that he was losing £4 weekly on *Commonweal* alone, and in 1889 he estimated his total socialist expenses as £500 annually, including the newspaper. (Glasier, pp. 194, 201) Moreover his pessimism was well founded; E.P. Thompson notes that from December 1887 to June 1889 its circulation had fallen from about 2,800 to about 2,300. (pp. 460-62)

[73] At the Chiswick Club; see his 7 February entry.

Feb[ruary] 16th. Sunday I spoke on a very cold windy (NE) morning at the Walham Green station:[74] the people listened well though the audience was not large about sixty at the most. I was busy all the afternoon entertaining Walker Scheu and his daughter[75] Tarleton and Tochatti; and Cunninghame Graham at last.

I lectured on 'Medieval England' to a good audience here in the evening: lecture rather 'young'.[76] Carruthers there: announced his going away in a fortnight to Venezuela again:[77] I am sorry as he is very useful here: also I like him.

Monday Council meeting very quiet and short: new branch at Walsall, a creation of Mahon's travels:[78] excited letter from the Glasgow branch: they have held a big meeting there Sunday in sympathy with the Lanarkshire miners:[79] more than 20,000 present they say; which as they collected twenty-four pounds (in coppers chiefly) seems likely. By the

---

[74] The Walham Green outdoor station was under the jurisdiction of the Hammersmith Branch; the 12 February *Commonweal* had announced a Mr Arnold as responsible for an 11.30 a.m. session on Sunday the 13th.

[75] Andreas Scheu's autobiography *Umsturzkeime* doesn't mention the names or birthdates of his three children, who had been left behind in Austria when he and his wife separated upon his departure for England in 1870. Scheu had continued to support his family from London; by 1887 his daughter would of course have been at least sixteen or seventeen, and could have visited her father independently.

[76] LeMire Ch, no.101, listed this as the first of three deliveries; the second on Wednesday 16 February, the third 22 March. This speech was the second in a trilogy on 'England, As It Was, As It Is, and As It May Be'.

[77] In 1883 John Carruthers had served the government of Venezuela as consulting engineer regarding the building of a railway from Puerto Cabello to Valencia, and he was now chief Venezuelan engineer for the London firm formed to construct the railway; later, from 1889 to 1891, he worked in Argentina.

[78] The 19 February *Commonweal*, p. 59, reported the meeting of 9 February at which the branch was formed in Walsall, an industrial town northwest of Birmingham. In a report in *Commonweal* of 26 February, 'Socialism in the Provinces', J.L. Mahon describes the chainmakers of Walsall and Cradley Heath as among the 'poorest paid slaves in this country', working 10–12 hours daily for 12 shillings a week, from which they were required to buy fuel for their forges.

[79] The Glasgow branch's report in *Commonweal*, 19 February, p. 61, spoke warmly of their success in 'Awakening the workers to a sense of the necessity of the Socialists' claim for a change in the basis of Society'.

way in the afternoon Bax called with Champion, who thinks of starting a new weekly, a private paper not so much a party journal as *Commonweal* and bigger, as he is to be backed by money.[80] He wanted my goodwill which he is welcome to; but I distrust the long endurance of a paper at all commercial, unless there is *plenty* of money at its back. Champion spoke in a friendly way and was quite open and reasonable; but seems out of spirits about the movement: he has been extremely over-sanguine about getting people to show their strength, which of course they don't do at present as soon as it looks dangerous, and so he is correspondingly depressed at the poor performance of the SDF in agitation lately.

By the way Bax tells me that the Clerkenwell affair was wholly and from the first the doing of the Clerkenwell and Marylebone Branches and that the executive disapproved of it, and were near to expelling the two sinning branches. That is all very well but after all is hardly fair; as it is but of a piece with the general advertising tactics of the SDF. Next Sunday they are going to have a 'church parade' at St Paul's: but unless they can get an enormous crowd, it will be a silly business, and if they do there will be a row; which got up in this way I think a mistake: take this for my word about this sort of thing: if a riot is quite spontaneous it does frighten the bourgeois even if it [is] but isolated; but planned riots or shows of force are no good unless in a time of action, when they are backed by the opinion of the people and are in point of fact indications of the rising tide.[81]

Again by the way at the Council meeting G.B. Shaw's letter was read accepting the championship against Bradlaugh, but with almost superfluous civility to him; and also saying that he could not bind himself to defend our Manifesto through thick and thin.[82] I expected an

---

[80] An ardent advocate of work towards labour representation in parliament and a legal eight-hour day, H. H. Champion was the owner of the Modern Press, which printed *Justice*. In May 1887 he founded *Common Sense*, and later published the *Labour Elector*. In 1885, Champion's provision of money from an unidentified source for SDF candidates created the 'Tory gold' scandal when the probable source was revealed as the Conservative agent Maltman Barry.

[81] Morris expressed his exasperation with SDF tactics on a number of occasions. For one such criticism of Hyndman's 'aim… to make the movement seem big; to frighten the powers that be with a turnip bogie which perhaps he almost believes in himself… ' see the biographical note on Hyndman.

outburst of opposition on this, as I thought rather needless proviso; but I suppose everybody saw that we mustn't withdraw our challenge, and Shaw is obviously the best man for the purpose.

Tuesday to Bax at Croydon[83] where we did our first article on Marx:[84] or rather he did it: I don't think I should ever make an economist even of the most elementary kind: but I am glad of the opportunity this gives me of hammering some Marx into myself.

Today I read the account in the paper (*Scotsman*) of the Glasgow meeting: it was very satisfactory. Muirhead a very mild and 'good' young man whom I met last year at Glasgow presided at one platform: this really is courageous of him, considering his mildness and his position, as he is something at the University.[85] By the way I forgot to say of last week that Parnell's amendment to the address was divided on last Thursday: I don't know if he expected to catch any Unionists by its 'moderation': if so he failed: for the majority against it was 106, a mere party division.[86]

---

[82] The letter, in Shaw's *Collected Letters*, 1874–97, pp. 164-65, concludes:
> I presume that your executive has duly weighed the fact that I am a member of the Fabian Society only, and am not bound by the manifesto of the Socialist League.

[83] Twelve miles south of central London, Croydon had a SL branch which met in Parker Road.

[84] The first part of this article, entitled 'Scientific Socialism', appeared in the 26 February *Commonweal*, and was later reprinted in *Socialism: Its Growth and Outcome*, London 1895; in a dry and reductive style it explains Marx's definitions of 'commodity', 'exchange', and 'money'.

[85] According to E.P. Thompson, R.F. Muirhead was a lecturer in mathematics at Glasgow University. (Thompson, p. 555) Glasier also comments on his courage in a letter in *Commonweal*:
> It is greatly to the credit of our comrades R.F. Muirhead, MA and Arch McLaren, MA, that they bravely came forward and took chairs at the platforms, as they are both well connected and run seriously the risk of damaging their academic careers. (19 February, p. 61)

[86] According to *The Times*, Parnell's amendment to the Queen's address was offered on Monday 7 February; the vote was actually not taken on Thursday, but on Friday 11 February; as Morris reported, the measure lost by 106 votes, 246 to 352. By his references to its moderation, Morris may have meant its general petitionary tone; Parnell wishes
> … humbly to represent to Her Majesty… that the remedy for the existing crisis in Irish affairs is not to be found in increased stringency of criminal procedure, or in the pursuit of such novel,

In the evening gave 'Medieval England' again at the League's place:[87] middling audience, no discussion: except a working man of the debating club type, not exactly a socialist I suppose; and a parson who preached sympathy between the classes: and Webb who shut him up. [88]

February 23rd. I had a sort of threat of gout the last days of last week, so kept myself quiet at home.[89] Sunday for same reason I did not speak out of doors. I went to Mitcham (the branch) on Sunday evening and spoke extemporary to them at their club-room, a tumble down shed opposite the grand new workhouse built by the Holborn Union: amongst the woeful hovels that make up the worse (and newer) part of Mitcham, which was once a pretty place with its old street and greens and lavender fields.[90] Except a German from Wimbledon (who was in the chair) and two others who looked like artisans of the painter or small builder-type, the audience was all made up of labourers and their wives: they were very quiet and attentive except one man who was courageous from liquor, and interrupted sympathetically: but I doubt if most of them understood anything I said; though some few of them showed that they did by applauding the points. I wonder sometimes

---

doubtful, and unconstitutional measures as have been taken by Her Majesty's Government in Ireland, but in such a reform of the law and the system of government as will satisfy the name and secure the confidence of the Irish people.

[87] LeMire Cal, p. 261.

[88] It's hard not to interpret Philip Webb's socialism as motivated in part by loyalty to his closest friend. That his politics may have been rather simplistic is suggested by the tone of his letter of 28 December 1884 from Florence (V & A Museum, Autograph):

… still no one must think that when capitalists are down on their marrow bones they will be for the people, they are a bad-bred lot, and the illgotten race must die out, for no good can come of them…

[89] In a letter to Jenny of 18 February he speaks of having had an alarm of gout rather than gout itself the previous week (BL Add. MS. 45,339, Kelvin 2:617); when writing to Glasier on 12 March he notes that he is not very well. (Autograph, WMorris Gal, Kelvin 2:626)

[90] Cf. Le Mire Cal, p. 261; the club room was at the corner of Merton Lane and Fountain Place. His 18 February letter to Jenny comments:

Tomorrow I lecture to our Mitcham branch, a creation of Kitz's; a rather tough lot of honest but poor people; I shall have to be as familiar and non-literary as I can be or they won't understand me. (BL Add. MS. 45,339, Kelvin 2:619)

if people will remember in times to come to what a depth of degradation the ordinary English workman has been reduced;[91] I felt very downcast amongst these poor people in their poor hutch whose opening I attended some three months back (and they were rather proud of it).[92] There were but about twenty-five present: Yet I felt as if I might be doing some good there: the branch is making way amongst a most wretched population.

Monday was Council-night again, and I attended. Poor Allman had been before the magistrate that day and fined forty s[hillings] and was sent to jail in default of payment: his offence was open-air preaching close to the meeting-place of the Hackney Branch:[93] so we are beginning our troubles early this year; which is a great nuisance; but I don't see what is to be done: we can't give up street-preaching in spite of what Bax and one

---

[91] I've been unable to identify the 'German from Wimbledon'. In contrast to Morris's depression, the *Commonweal* Mitcham branch report signed by S.G. noted enthusiastically that:

> In the evening in our club-room, comrade Morris lectured to a very large audience on 'Monopoly', and met with an enthusiastic reception. Eden, Harrison, Gregory and others took part in the discussion. We closed as usual with singing. Four new members made.

[92] *Commonweal* reported its opening on 24 October 1886; Frank Kitz's branch report for 20 October notes enthusiastically that:

> Our Mitcham club room was a dilapidated ruinous shed, which by purely voluntary efforts on the part of our Mitcham and Merton comrades, has been transferred into a comfortable club room... . (p. 247)

[93] The 26 February *Commonweal*, p. 71, recounted Allman's biased trial and spirited self-defence:

> Allman pointed out the injustice of the police attacking only Socialists and no one else; and that it was only when a few working men bound themselves together to point out to their fellows how they were robbed that the ruling class put this old law into force. There were hundreds of meetings held every evening, not by Socialists, that really did cause obstructions, that were never interfered with, which showed the partiality of the police. Meetings were held three times a-week by a ranter five yards from where he was arrested for speaking, but the police only looked on.

Allman's heavy fine seemed a direct result of his two previous convictions; after hearing that Allman had been fined at Dod Street and Stratford, the judge Mr Hannay 'said that under those circumstances he would inflict the full penalty of 40s. or a month'. A Hyde Park demonstration was held on 28 March to celebrate Allman's release.

or two others say about its uselessness: Yet the police if they persist can put us down; and unless we can get up a very good case of causeless interference on their part, and consequent presumption of unfairness against us, we shall not be able to enlist the radical clubs on our side, which is our only chance. At the Council we agreed not to pay Allman's fine, as he cried out loudly against it; and I believe meant it as he is a courageous little man; and is single and wretchedly poor: it was agreed that a committee should see to getting up a free speech demonstration in Hackney.[94] I may note here for the benefit of well-to-do West Enders that the police are incredibly rough and brutal to the poor people in the East End; and that they treated Allman very ill. Charles was hauled over the coals at this Council meeting for having written to *Justice* in a way that seemed to imply an official communication, and a disclaimer of officiality was ordered to be written.[95] Bax brought the matter on, and I thought at first that it was a piece of eager party spirit on his part, as Charles belongs to the quasi-Anarchist-section: but I saw that Charles had made a mistake, so I did not oppose. The occasion of the letter was a paragraph in *Justice* jeering at Mahon, who is on a stumping mission in the country for his change of front on the parliamentary matter.[96] I

---

[94] *Commonweal*, 26 February, announced that the Hackney Branch planned to hold a Sunday meeting in the Broadway (London Fields) to publicise the difficulties of socialist propaganda, and the 5 March issue reported that at the meeting speeches by H. Graham and David Nicoll were followed by passage of a resolution protesting the sentencing of Allman, and supporting free speech.

[95] Henry Charles's letter appeared in the 19 February *Justice*, p. 3 and read:
Comrade, — In reference to the first of your Tell-tale Straws, pray permit me to correct your statement.
1. John L. Mahon had not been sent as an emissary of the Socialist League to the Provinces.
2. The principles of the Socialist League are now as they were at the formation of the League, opposed to Socialists adopting political action in the sense you understand political action.
3. The deplorable fact that comrade Mahon has within the last six months somewhat changed his ideas does not necessarily induce all other members of the Socialist League to follow suit.
I am, Comrade, yours fraternally,
H. Charles
[96] Later in the year J.L. Mahon would become more clearly parliamentarian, but his *Commonweal* articles reporting the northern trip still emphasised

may as well say here that my intention is if possible to prevent the quarrel coming to a head between the two sections parliamentary and anti-parliamentary and which are pretty much commensurate with the collectivists and Anarchists: and this because I believe there would be a good many who would join the Anarchist side who are not really Anarchists, and who would be useful to us: indeed I doubt if except for one or two Germans we have any real Anarchists amongst us:[97] and I don't want to see a lot of enthusiastic men who are not very deep in Socialist doctrines[98] driven off for a fad of the more pedantic part of the Collectivist section.

We had an answer from Bradlaugh about the debate; rather doubtful I think: however we shall try to carry it through. Donald and Barker (the secretary) appointed to see to it.

Yesterday all day long with Bax trying to get our second article on Marx together:[99] a very difficult job: I hope it may be worth the trouble.

[Facing page contains article by William Morris; see appendix, 'Newspaper Articles Inserted in the *Socialist Diary*.' Morris's gloss reads, 'A railway proposed from Windermere to Ambleside intending to go

---

the need for political agitation in a wider Socialist frame:

> [Of Nottingham:] There is plenty of Socialist feeling in the town but the disorganised and dilatory way in which the propaganda has been conducted, has estranged this feeling from the Socialist bodies. The cause of this state of affairs is, in my opinion, that from the first the movement had too much politics and too little Socialism in it. The social and economic aspect of the propaganda was over-shadowed by the political: the result being that a very superficial and spurious kind of Socialism was spread abroad, that died out when the election heat cooled off. (26 February, p. 69)

Late in 1887 Mahon founded a North of England Socialist Federation pledged to work with both the SDF and SL; for a discussion of his activities, see Thompson, pp. 464-79.

[97] The real anarchists to which he refers were probably Victor Dave and the Whitfield Street anarchists, see notes 55–58.

[98] What exactly Morris feared from the anti-parliamentarian SL members (Lane, Kitz, Mowbray, Mainwaring, Nicoll) is not clear — perhaps more pronounced advocacy of demonstrations, strikes, violence, and open threats to the government. Anarchist sympathies within the SL were largely confined to London (though the Welsh Mainwaring was an exception); provincial branches favoured more electoral and trade union activity.

[99] On 'Money', *Commonweal*, 12 March, p. 82.

right through the Lake Country in time / *Pall Mall Gazette* Feb[ruary] 22 1887.][100]

News of the German Elections today: the Socialists seem to be going to lose seats (and no wonder considering Bismarck's iron fist) but they are gaining numbers according to the voting.[101]

Sparling went down on Monday night to Reading to try to found a branch, after the good reception which he and Carruthers had there last week: but it was a dead failure:[102] a good many had given their names to attend, but when it came to the scratch 'with one consent they all began to make excuse': I note this because it is characteristic of the present stage of the movement; for as abovesaid there was plenty of agreement at the meetings we have held there. This hanging-back is partly fear of being boycotted by the masters; but chiefly from dislike to organisation, for a question which the 'respectable' political parties ignore; and also fear of anything like revolt or revolution.

March 3ʳᵈ. Last Thursday to Ways and Means Committee but nothing done there because of a meeting of the Commune Celebration Committee, at which the Autonomy group (of unrespectable Anarchists) had sent people to make a mess of our arrangements; wanting us to give up our meeting and join them on a meeting the day after, though they knew that our bills were out and that we had hired the hall; I think I have mentioned that this section of Anarchists have a quarrel on with the others, and just mention this trifling matter to illustrate it: there were delegates from other bodies there who, not understanding the affair were for 'giving way to' the Autonomy group, who only number about seventeen persons, and include Reuss among them, whom we expelled as a spy.

---

[100] The speeches of Messrs Louther and Labouchere to which Morris refers appeared in *The Times* of 18 February.

[101] Despite repressive measures and the imprisonment of its leaders, the German Social Democratic party had rapidly gained adherents, claiming over 300,000 members in 1881 and over 1,400,000 in 1890. In an attempt to blunt its influence and justify domestic suppression of socialists, Bismarck had introduced some limited social reforms and exploited supposed threats of war. J. Sketchley published an article 'Law and Order in Germany' in the 5 March *Commonweal*.

[102] No reference to the Reading meeting appears in *Commonweal*. Morris alludes to Luke 14:18, 'And they all with one consent began to make excuse.'

Sunday Shaw here to meet Th[eodore] Watts,[103] and was very amusing. I urged him to get on with the promised handbook of Socialism:[104] he pleaded poverty, and gave us a comical account of the adventures of a literary man among the publishers: he writes slowly and carefully all he does, which certainly doesn't *pay*.

As to Sunday meetings of our branch: Walham Green had a sort of debate, with a gathering of the Primrose Leaguers to oppose;[105] but went off pretty well, though a sort of thing which is a great nuisance.

I spoke at Beadon Road; fair attendance of the usual kind, I met a posse of horse police going to St Paul's apropos of the SDF's church-parade there;[106] and there were also a crowd of Police at the metropolitan station.

Mrs Wilson in evening; the lecture good with the usual anarchist twang in it:[107] she was somewhat heckled by Beasley and Carruthers; the latter speaking very well. Her defence was not strong.

The SDF Church Parade went off well: they ought not to spoil it by having inferior ones at small churches now; but should change the entertainment, which remark points to the weak side of their tactics: they must always be getting up some fresh excitement, or else making the thing stale and at last ridiculous; so that they are rather in the position of a hard-pressed manager of a theatre — what are they to do next?

---

[103] In a letter of 25 February to Jenny, Morris notes that he plans to entertain G.B. Shaw and Watts (Theodore Watts-Dunton) the next Sunday, 27 February, because the latter wanted to meet Shaw. (Kelvin 2:623) Neither man is mentioned in the autobiographical writings, published letters, or standard biographies of the other, and the meeting seems to have been of little consequence.

[104] Perhaps these essays evolved into Shaw's two contributions to the *Fabian Essays* of 1889. One of the latter, 'The Transition to Social Democracy', was written in 1888 while Shaw visited Kelmscott Manor.

[105] The spring primrose became associated by Conservatives with the memory of Benjamin Disraeli's death on 19 April 1881; in 1883 the Primrose League was founded to support the Conservative Party principles.

[106] This was the 27 February SDF parade, which went discreetly unannounced in the 26 February *Commonweal*.

[107] According to the 5 March *Commonweal*, she lectured on 'Authority and Revolt', and the branch report notices that 'The Anarchist theory underlying an interesting discourse was criticised by comrades Beasley, Carruthers, Morris, and Radford, who were mainly concerned with the difficulty of finding how the everyday affairs of a community could be conducted without the rule... of either majority or minority'.

Good meeting on this Sunday at Edinburgh in favour of the miners got up by the League and the SDF.[108] All went much as in Glasgow.

Went to the Council meeting on Monday;[109] the meeting *rather* inclined to quarrel. The Charles letter-affair brought up again as I knew it would be, but Charles himself moved the dropping of it. A good deal of talk about the open-air-free-speech business: we are to have it out next Monday, when I shall take some trouble to get them to be reasonable but don't expect to succeed:[110] the matter of the monthly meeting of members is also to come up next Monday: so we shall have a pretty lively time of it. It really is a pity that the said meeting should drop; but holding it on the Monday means knocking off one council meeting a month, and I don't think we have a right to do that. Lane's journey to Paris as our delegate by the way turned out rather a joke:[111] the Feast he was to go to was a paying business, and though a delegate he was received with no hospitality; though Lafargue knows him and speaks English; the meeting a poor one. Altogether Lane, and Charles (who went with him) came back with a very poor impression of the Guesdist or orthodox collectivist section there; and after making all deductions for their Anarchist prejudices, I suspect their impression is right, and that Bax exaggerates their importance.[112]

---

[108] The 27 February Edinburgh demonstration of the SDL and SL to express sympathy with striking Scottish miners was reported in the 5 March *Commonweal*, p. 77.

[109] On 13 February; see 19 February *Commonweal*, p. 61.

[110] Morris had expressed his views on the distracting effects of this agitation in a letter to Glasier of the preceding 16 August:

> You will see that we are in hot water again with the police here, and for my part I think it a great nuisance. It is after all a side issue, and I grudge everything that takes people's attention off the true economical and social issues which are the only things of importance… . (WMorris Gal, Kelvin 2:565-66)

The collection of fines and creation of publicity to support arrested comrades had consumed much of the League's energies during the past year.

[111] Morris had encouraged Joseph Lane to serve as the League's representative to a Paris congress of international socialists (letter to Lane, 17 February, 1887, BL Add. MS. 46,345, Kelvin 2:616). Morris paid the expenses of the trip. Like the British movement, French socialism was factionalised between anarchists, mutualists (Syndicalists), collectivists, and parliamentarians (Possibilists).

[112] The Guesdist Parti Ouvrier, founded by Jules Guesde (1845–1922) in 1875–76, upheld orthodox Marxist collectivism in competition with Blanquist and

---

That implies that, though the Socialist idea is widespread in France, there is nothing scarcely of an organised party there: I forgot to say that on Monday Shaw sent in a letter very clear and precise statement of the terms on which he would debate with Bradlaugh:[113] the latter cannot say that they are unreasonable, and can scarcely draw out of it without discredit.

Tuesday I spent with Bax doing the next Marx article, which went easier:[114] as a contrast I had a long spell with Carruthers, to whom I went to take leave of him as he is going back to Venezuela and he read me the second (and important) chapter of his *Political Economy*, which is by the standard of Marx quite heretical.[115] It seemed to me clear and reasonable; and at any rate has this advantage, that it sets forth the antagonism of classes in the nakedest manner: the workman is nothing but part of the capitalist machinery; and if he is rebellious is to be treated like a rebellious spade would be, or say a troublesome piece of land.

March 9th. The ways-and-means committee meeting on Thursday last was swamped by the meeting of delegates about the Commune celebration: the Autonomy people were represented and inclined to give way: also the SDF had written to Brocher (who with a Socialist Union man had been told off to arrange matters with the other groups

<hr>

Proudhonist factions. Guesde edited *Égalité* and was a close collaborator of Paul Lafargue, Marx's son-in-law. Presumably the Guesdists were especially cool to Lane as an anarcho-communist.

[113] See Shaw's *Collected Letters*, pp. 165-66.

[114] This was 'Scientific Socialism — Conversion of Capital into Money', published in the 19 March *Commonweal*, p. 104.

[115] It's hard to be completely certain what this was. Carruther's *Political Economy of Socialism: Lecture Read Before the Hammersmith Branch of the Socialist League*, is an undated sixteen-page pamphlet, listed in the National Union Catalogue as '1885?' If this date is correct, it seems strange that Morris would be learning of its contents for the first time in a conversation with his friend two years later. The pamphlet was reviewed by *Commonweal* on 20 September 1890, and listed there as published by the Hammersmith Branch SL, Kelmscott House, so it seems more likely that it was printed sometime between the dates of the *Diary* reference and the review. This pamphlet seems a more likely candidate for Morris' reference than Chapter 2 of the 1883 *Communal and Commercial Economy*, the contents of which were already published. Like *Communal and Commercial Economy*, *The Political Economy of Socialism* contained the description of worker-as-machinery which attracted Morris.

including the SDF)[116] asking us to join them in a big hall and have but one meeting. This was all very well but I saw from the letter that they simply meant that we should attend their meeting and swell their triumph: which indeed I thought we had better do, if they would come only a little way to meet us. The other groups were harmonious.

On this night there was a good row in the House between the Government and the Parnellites backed by a few radicals:[117] Hicks-Beach the Irish Secretary lost his temper and threatened the Irish members roundly, and they gave back as good as they took or better. For it is clear that the Government is in a shaky condition. The Union Liberals are beginning to see that the cat is going to jump the other way: Trevelyan made a speech at Devonshire House this week as good as renouncing the Tory alliance:[118] so it seems the Liberal party is to be remitted on the basis of a Compromise Home Rule Bill; which will last as long as the Irish find convenient. Meantime the Government are threatening a very harsh coercion bill:[119] indeed I shouldn't wonder if they were not to make it as stiff as possible in order to ensure their own defeat, and then were to appeal to the Country on the ground of law and order. All this is blessed bread to us even the reunion of the Liberal party; because after all that means the Whigs still retaining their hold of it, the stripping it more and more of anything which could enable it to pose as a popular party; while on the other hand it cripples the radicals, and takes away all chance of their forming a popular party underneath the more advanced Liberals: so that in politics the break up of the old parties and the formation of a strong reactionary party goes on apace.

---

[116] Gustave Brocher, according to Quail (pp. 16, 48) a contributor to Henry Seymour's *The Anarchist* and an organiser of the London Social Revolutionary and Anarchist Congress of July 1881, was to lecture at the Hammersmith Branch SL on 24 April on the Belgian 'rational socialist' Jean Colins; see Morris's final entry.

[117] Argument between the Parnellites and the Government erupted on Thursday 3 March over the issue of Civil Service estimates of £30,960 supplementary pay for the constabulary of Ireland. (*The Times*, 4 March, pp. 6-8)

[118] Devonshire House was the Piccadilly London palace of Lord Hartington, head of the Liberal Unionist faction, and therefore a central Unionist meeting place.

[119] In the debate of 3 March, the government did threaten a harsher Coercion Bill. Under Balfour's guidance, the 1887 Crimes Act was finally passed during the summer.

The morning after this row, lo Hicks-Beach has resigned on the score of 'ill-health'![120] Balfour the new secretary; though it matters little who among the Tories takes the place.[121]

Sunday I went to the new premises of the Hoxton Branch (the Labour Emancipation League) to lecture:[122] I rather liked it: a queer little no-shaped slip cut off from some workshop or other neatly whitewashed, with some innocent decoration obviously by the decorator members of the branch: all very poor but showing signs of sticking to it: the room full of a new audience of the usual type of attenders at such places: all working men except a parson in the front row, and perhaps a clerk or two, the opposition represented by a fool of the debating club type; but our men glad of any opposition at all. I heard that our branch lecture was a wretched failure.[123] The fact is our branch which was very vigorous a little time ago, is sick now; the men want some little new thing to be doing or they get slack in attendance. I must try to push them together a bit.

I attended the Council meeting on Monday. It was in the end quarrelsome;[124] Donald captious and obviously attacking Lane, who was

---

[120] Actually, Hicks-Beach announced his resignation on Saturday afternoon, and it was not reported in *The Times* until Monday 7 March. He resigned on the grounds that he needed cataract surgery; Morris's skepticism was probably unjustified, since he returned to Parliament after the operation.

[121] Alexander James Balfour, the Conservative prime minister 1902–5, was then Secretary for Scotland and served as Irish Secretary from 1887–91. *The Times* was correct in its editorial of 8 March when it predicted that:

If we judge Mr Balfour's character aright, he will not shrink from the disagreeable duty of sternly enforcing the law. (p. 9)

[122] 'How We Live and How We Might Live,' at Hoxton Branch, Labour Emancipation League, 2 Crondel Street, New North Rd, Hoxton, Le Mire Cal., p. 261.

[123] The 5 March *Commonweal* had announced a lecture by A.K. Donald on 'Political Economy from the Socialist Standpoint'. Both Donald's personal manner and his parliamentarianism may have alienated Hammersmith Branch SL members.

[124] The present issue of contention was whether the 1887 Conference would reverse its antiparliamentarianism. Compare a letter from Philip Webb to Charles Faulkner, Tuesday 8 March:

I cannot say that my intellect is allowed to rust for last night at our Council meeting there was more cantankerous criticism than enough and more angry answer (sic) than would serve for a board meeting of a vestry. (WMorris Gal, J551)

very raw and sore: and at last over some nothing about the Commune meeting the latter resigned his place on it, and everything seemed at a deadlock:[125] then I must needs flyte them, which I did with a good will, pitching into both parties. As to details it is worth noting that we are getting noisy in our Hyde Park meeting, and the police are interfering: no doubt, as Donald states, the police are getting all this up there in order to rouse public feeling so that they may put down speaking there altogether: I note by the way that there is no doubt that the police take careful notes of the Socialist speakers now. We passed a resolution practically bidding our speakers not to draw on quarrels with the police: though I doubt if they will heed it often: as some of them are ambitious of figuring as heroes in this 'free-speech' business.[126] This is a pity; as if the police stick to it, they can of course beat us in the long run: and we have more out-o-door stations already than we can man properly already.

The Conference — Donald moved that it be held on Whit Sunday: Lane moved for the August holiday, on the ground of the financial statement not being likely or possible to be ready at the earlier date: I supported him on the true grounds that I don't want to hurry the branches over the parliament-non-parliament question.[127] We were beaten: which Lane took hardly.

Bradlaugh writes declining to modify his conditions (though no one could understand what they were); however we shall give way in order to pin him; which by the way we shall fail to do.

---

[125] Disputes over financial reliability and the contents and distribution of *Commonweal* resulted from and intensified Council debates on ideology. The Lane-Donald antagonism became yet more acrimonious later in the year. Amsterdam IISH letters record that Donald attacked *Commonweal* for dullness (7 July 1887, Donald to Council, IIHS 1295), and Lane accused Donald of pocketing £15 collected for the miners (source R. Goldstein).

[126] The 19 March *Commonweal* reported the following Council resolution: 'That the speakers at Hyde Park invite the audience to keep within the railings so as not to obstruct the foot-paths; and that all members of the League attending such meetings be careful not to obstruct the foot-ways on such occasions'.

[127] The 26 March *Commonweal* announced the Conference for Whitsunday, 29 May, at 13 Farringdon Road, EC1.

March 21st. Sunday 13th I went to lecture in a queer little den for the Hackney branch, a street out of Goldsmiths' Row, Hackney Road, a very miserable part of the East End of course:[128] meeting small almost all members I suspect: one oldish man a stranger, a railway labourer who opposed in a friendly way gave me an opportunity of explaining to the audience various points which I expect; also a fresh opportunity (if I needed it) of gauging the depths of ignorance and consequent incapacity of following an argument which possesses the uneducated averagely stupid person. I found we had had a bad meeting at home the next morning.[129] On the Monday I went to Edinburgh[130] and lectured at the

---

[128] 'Monopoly', at 23 Audrey St, Goldsmith Row, Hackney, E2, Le Mire Cal., p. 261, and checklist, p. 309 no. 103. In 1887 this was a new lecture, which Morris delivered frequently during the next three years; it appears in *CW*, vol. XXIII pp. 238-54.

[129] Hubert Bland, a Fabian, had spoken on 'What State Interference Means'.

[130] Morris was somewhat exasperated at the prospect of two disconnected trips north within a month's time; he wrote to Jenny on 9 March:

> I find, much to my disgust, that I shall have to make a flying visit to Edinburgh next Monday. It seems I made the appointment last year, and of course forgot about it, and they stupidly didn't remind me of it or I would have made my Glasgow visit which now comes off later fit in with it. However I don't mind except for the expense. A long railway journey with a book to read and Homer, and the window is a kind of rest to me after all; for I will not go by night, which is beastly. (BL Add. MS. 45,339, Kelvin 2:625)

At the time the Edinburgh trip took about ten hours by train; according to Bradshaw's *Railway Almanack* for that year, Morris could have left from Kings Cross on the Great Northern Railway at 5.15 a.m. and arrived in Edinburgh at 3.40 p.m., and there were several alternate possibilities.

Free Tron Hall was at 4 Park Street; Morris lectured on 14 March on 'Socialism: The End and the Means', to a meeting sponsored by the Scottish Land and Labour League chaired by the Rev. John Glasse. On Tuesday 15 March the *Scottish Leader* printed a lengthy report on p. 7, col. 5, 'Mr William Morris on Socialism,' including an approximately 1000 word summary of his speech. Morris spoke of the Unionist-Tory alliance as one founded on fear, then delivered his familiar prediction:

> This change of parties would go on until there were none left but the Socialists on the one hand, and the haters of the people on the other. Then would come the struggle, and whatever form that struggle took, it would not be a long one. It would be sure to result in victory for Socialism, and upon that victory the new world

lower Tron hall; the audience was but slender in numbers:[131] there being counter-attractions again, two important meetings being on the same night: one under the same roof, and so near that its applause interfered with my oratory. The audience however was both attentive and intelligent and very enthusiastic: the opposition came only from two persons, one a conservative secularist apparently who seemed to speak well, but was so indistinct that I couldn't really catch the thread of his argument; the other an old fellow named Bone and nicknamed the 'Bone of Contention' who goes about opposing everywhere, a wooden creature, but not quite stupid.[132] An SDF man spoke very well, also one of ours no less well. On the whole a satisfactory meeting.

In fact things seem on the rise in Scotland.[133] In Edinburgh our branch is doing better, though the SDF are more active, as they have more working-men amongst them; our people are on quite good terms

---

would rise to crown the efforts of the past, and to stimulate to new efforts in the future. (Loud applause)

The *Edinburgh Evening News* published a similar report on the same day, p. 2, col. 3.

[131] The *Scottish Leader* article had commented on the moderate attendance: 'The Audience, though not so large as the reputation of the lecturer might have led the promoters to expect, was by no means a small one.' (p. 7) The *Edinburgh Evening News* noted, 'There was only a small attendance.' (p. 2)

[132] On the evening of 14 April Morris wrote to Jenny that a meeting on 5 April had passed their resolution despite hostility,

... after a rather stormy debate, owning to the stupidity of a cut and dried opponent one Job Bone, who always opposes everything and is known in Edinburgh as the 'Bone of Contention'. (Henderson, *Letters*, p. 270; Kelvin 2:642)

A *Commonweal* report of an Edinburgh meeting on 18 March 1888 described a 'brisk discussion', in which 'the indefatigable Job Bone, a pillar of capitalism well known to Socialist lecturers, was severely handled.' (*Commonweal*, 24 March)

[133] This of course resulted from the strike by the Federation of Scottish Miners. On Friday 20 May, within a month of Morris's entry, the miners voted for negotiation — essentially an admission of defeat. Here too the SDF's parliamentariansm was popular with workingmen; Thompson contrasts Mahon's striking success when campaigning in eastern Scotland on a parliamentary programme, later in 1887, with the SL's loss of at least four provincial branches after the 1888 split over election campaigning. (pp. 462, 474)

with them: best of all the general feeling of advanced political people is turning our way there. Glasse proclaimed himself a socialist and active, at the lecture, and said he was going to join the League:[134] this means a good deal as to the turn of public opinion, as his position*[135] forces him to be cautious. Glasse and I went to Roslin the next day;[136] a beautiful glen-ny landscape much spoiled temporarily by the remains of last week's snow, and permanently by the misery of Scotch building and a manufactory or two. The chapel strange indeed; unquestionably romantic; but the work coarse and quite lacking the deft skill and crispness of medieval work; the romance laid on with a trowel, as if by an amateur determined to be romantic; and all this before the end of the fifteenth century![137]

Back I went to London by night train and waking at Hatfield[138] found the whole country under a white blanket of snow, and the trees like a father-Christmas toy: that day (the Tuesday) everybody told me had been the blackest and nastiest day ever seen in London.

---

[134] Thompson considers the Rev. John Glasse (not to be confused with the anarchist Henry Glasse) one of the League's few steady provincial allies. (p. 555) Several of Morris's letters to Glasse were reprinted by R. Page Arnot in *Unpublished Letters of William Morris*, Labour Monthly Pamphlet, 1951 Series, no. 6. According to Arnot (p. 3), Glasse had been a member of the SDF before joining the SL. When visiting Edinburgh Morris stayed with Glasse and his wife at their home at 16 Tantallon Place, and he invited Glasse to visit him in London as the Edinburgh Branch's Conference delegate in May, 1887. Glasse declined, and after the Conference Morris wrote him a long letter defining his position. He seems to have considered Glasse a moderate ally, who was anxious above all to avoid another split within the League.

[135] * minister of the old Grey-friars Church (Morris's note)

[136] Cassell's *Old and New Edinburgh* (London 1887) describes Roslin, a town directly south of the city, as 'a retreat of rural quietness, and the abode of workers in the bleaching-fields and powder-mills.' (p. 352) The latter may be the 'manufactories' which Morris mentions. Bartholomew's 1912 *Survey Atlas of Scotland*, plate 62, shows a carpet mill and river nearby.

[137] Cassell's guide notes that the chapel was founded in 1446, and quotes a historian who describes its baroque ornamentation:

> It is impossible to designate the architecture of this building by any given or familiar term, for the variety and eccentricity of its parts are not to be defined by any words of common acceptation. (p. 350)

[138] Hatfield is about thirty miles north of London.

CELEBRATING THE COMMUNE.

The building in South-place, Finsbury, where Mr. Conway used to lecture, threw open its doors last night to the Socialists to enable them to celebrate the anniversary of the Commune. To-day is the true date. Last night was but the eve of the outbreak ; but to-day the building will be wanted again for the same purpose by the more Anarchical section of the party. To-night will be for denunciation, last night was more especially for discussion by the milder-mannered men and women of the party. Prince Krapotkine's name was on the hand-bills, with the names of William Morris, Mrs. Wilson, Mrs. Annie Besant, and a few others. Of Mrs. Wilson not everybody outside the ranks may have heard. She is a convinced Socialist, and the wife of a professional man, and she has given up all the property she possesses in her own right, and the pleasure of living ; in a fine house, to live like her brothers and sisters of the proletariat in the humblest style. The meeting was advertised for eight o'clock, and before that time the hall was nearly filled. A little later it was quite full, floor and galleries. The audience were of the artisan class. They were very decently dressed, and up to about ten o'clock, when our representative left, they were perfectly well behaved. They were quiet thoughtful-looking men and women—for many of the men were accompanied by their wives, and some by their babies. The societies more especially represented were the Socialist League, to which Mr. Morris belongs ; the Fabian Society, a sort of Socialist Parliament which meets twice a month at Willis's Rooms, and sometimes at the private houses of members ; and the Communist Club in Tottenham-street, with its three or four affiliated institutions of the same kind. This is sometimes called the German Club, and it deserves attention as one of the strange growths of this strange time. It numbers about three hundred members ; it rents capacious premises ; it publishes a weekly paper in the German tongue. With these was the Autonomie Group, of a more marked Anarchist tendency, that almost proved to be the little leaven leavening the whole lump.

A humble sort of man, named Lane, who acted as chairman, spoke first. He took his station on the platform with a few dirty red flags to right and left of him, looking dirtier in the dim light of the hall—why is Freethought of every description usually so sparing of its gas ?—and he made a short introductory speech. He dropped his h's recklessly, as might have been expected ; and we only mention it to show that he was in character. His theme was that the cause of Communism, though crushed in 1871, was stronger than ever to-day, and that the Commune was a great advance on all previous revolutions, because it was social ; while the others were only political. The next revolution, in like manner, would be a great advance on that.

One Frank Kitz followed him, another man of the same educational rank, but fluent and measured, and with a clear sense of what he wanted to say. He was denunciatory, but always within bounds, and he could be quite angry without foaming at the mouth. He was very angry with the English Press ; it pandered to the capitalist class ; it was a moral policeman doing the dirty work of society. He was angry, too, with " the cowardly English Trades-Unionists "—there was loud applause when he said this. What the Commune died for was to mend such misery as the misery of our unemployed. This was the note of doctrine for the whole meeting ; whenever a speaker repeated this, or something like it, he was sure of his cheer. " Before many years have passed," he said, in conclusion, " we shall begin to handle the wealth which is the produce of our hands." This earned him frantic applause. Then a young fellow, who looked like a clerk, said something. He was announced as " Macdonald," and his accent did not belie the promise of his name. He cared little whether the Commune was right or wrong in its acts ; its intentions were so good. A German, who spoke in his own language, said they celebrated the 18th March only as one of the Revolutions which, taking them in their entirety, must remain the true business of the proletariat until they won their rights.

Mrs. Wilson followed, as representative of the " Freedom Group." Mrs. Wilson is a slender person, bordering on middle age, but on the right side of the border, dressed becomingly in black, and with hair trained forward in an ordered mass to form a sort of frame of jet for the thin, thoughtful face. The type is the South Kensington or British Museum art-student, the æsthete with " views," and Mrs. Wilson quite realised it as to the views. She was decidedly Anarchical. Is it superfluous to say here that Anarchy stands with these doctrinaires for a sort of philosophic horror of all government, even of the government of the good ? Compulsion, headship, law, in a word, as such, they hold to be bad. We are to take to the right and good as ducks take to the water by the guidance of our own natural impulses. Mrs. Wilson did not say all this, but that meaning underlay her words. What she did say was delivered with great clearness of enunciation, with great purity of accent, with a certain appearance of effort, not to say of fatigue, as though the hall taxed her voice beyond its powers, and with the monotonous calm that is perhaps the most common outward sign of the born fanatic. She was quite womanly and ladylike to use the good old-fashioned word. As she now and then refreshed her memory from her manuscript she exhibited a certain hesitation that had the effect at least of timidity, and that did not misbecome her sex and her evident good breeding. The great fault of the Commune, she said, was that it tried to form a Government, a regular orderly administration, with arbitrary powers ; the great virtue of the Commune was that it brought men and women together into simpler social relations and truer brotherhood.

Inserted clipping on Paris Commune Celebration,
March 18th, 1887 *Daily News* (British Library Add MS 45,335)

92

In the society of the future the typical bad man would not be the passionate man, nor the coward, nor even the lazy man. It would be the man who tried to force others to obey or to serve him. If it had not been for the foolish attempt of the Commune to set up a sort of legal government, the people, left to their own best impulses, would at once have seized their property, the property of the workers, stored up in the Bank of France. This was no joke on the part of Mrs. Wilson—not so much as a paradox. She said it as though, in her opinion, it were absolutely self-evident. It was too much for another Scotchman who followed, Citizen Donald. He argued, with some warmth, against fantastic notions, and he thought the thing the Communists most wanted was better drill. "If we are going to fight, let us have weapons in our hands." The applause with which this was greeted showed that the audience had begun to feel comfortable again, and that Mrs. Wilson had been only half understood. Soon after up rose "Krapotkine," amid tremendous applause. "He is a Prince, you know, in his own country," whispered a man in the audience to a friend. He looked every inch a savant. He was in faultless black from head to foot, save, of course, at the neck, though little was to be seen thereof for the great beard that swept half-way down the breast. His bald head seemed to give additional height to his brow. He might have stepped out of a scientific soirée at St. Petersburg, and at the very moment that he stood on this platform, no doubt, dozens of gentlemen almost exactly like him were explaining bi-metalism or the earthquake to fair listeners at soirées in the Russian capital. Prince Krapotkine, too, was explaining the earthquake in his way, but it was a visitation of a kind unknown to seismography. It was a vibration that was "to shake Europe all through by the end of this century." He, like Mrs. Wilson, had the well-bred air. He was emphatic without being noisy, but perhaps he was to some extent held in check by his imperfect command of our accent. His literary English left little or nothing to be desired. As a piece of construction, his speech bore few traces of foreign origin; for the rest, it was piquantly outlandish in almost every other word. He waved off the applause, or, rather, took it, with thanks, like a subscription "for those who now suffer in the gaols." He, too, was anarchical in his general drift. He admired the manner of the seizure of the guns at Montmartre. The workmen did it themselves, without leaders. The Commune had realised little or nothing in the Socialist way, and nevertheless it had a profound interest for everyone. A popular movement was not to be judged by what it had accomplished, but by its aspirations. The most shocking thing he had ever seen was a testimonial from a number of wealthy men in Paris to the keeper of a restaurant, to the effect that he had never suffered them to want a good dinner all through the siege; and this "while the others were glad to buy a rat for tenpence"—the Prince's only slip. If the workmen of Paris had only seized the empty workshops as they seized the guns, it would have been well; but, unfortu-

nately, they waited for an order from their Government that never came. In the coming revolution, they must, first of all, take possession of property, and when they have done that, "no one will ever again sleep on London Bridge." The applause was frantic at the beginning, middle, and end of this speech, and it broke forth afresh when a tall, handsome woman, with her dark hair and complexion set off in effective contrast by a gown of reddish velvet, came to the front of the platform. It was Mrs. Besant. She was just as calm in manner, and as violent in speech, as most of the others; and with her balanced oration, so far at least as our experience of it went, this singular meeting came to an end.

Thursday (17) came off our Commune celebration at last and turned out very successful:[139] Kitz Kropotkin Mrs Wilson Donald, all made very good speeches: only Mrs Wilson's was too much of a lecture, and she really went too far with her Utopian Anarchist superstition: Donald rather attacked her, and fairly.[140] I spoke last and, to my great vexation and shame, *very* badly; fortunately I was hoarse, and so I hope they took that for an excuse; though it wasn't the reason; which was that I tried to be literary and original, and so paid for my egotism.[141] However it didn't

---

[139] The International Celebration of the Paris Commune was held at South Place Chapel, Finsbury, EC, at 8 p.m. Despite the hostilities recorded by Morris's diary, *Commonweal* announced an impressive number of sponsors:

> The Societies taking part are: Fabian Society; Socialist Union; Socialist League; International Workingmen's Clubs of Berners Street, Cleveland Hall, 49 Tottenham Street, and 23 Princes Square; Autonomie Group; Freedom Group; Scandinavian Group; and FrancoItalian Group.

Besides speeches in French, German, and Italian, in addition to those Morris mentions English speeches were delivered by Annie Besant, Peter Kropotkin, Joseph Lane, and J.R. Macdonald. *The Times*, *Pall Mall Gazette*, and *Daily News* all carried reports of the meeting.

[140] Essentially Morris expresses here a more moderate form of the *Pall Mall's* criticism of Charlotte Wilson:

> 'The great fault of the Commune was that it tried to form a Government, a regular orderly Administration, with arbitrary powers; the great virtue of the Commune was that it brought men and women together into simpler social relations and truer brotherhood;' This [is a] literal quotation from the speech of a certain Mrs Wilson, who appears to be otherwise an estimable lady, at the meeting at South Place last night to commemorate the Commune. The Commune has certainly had many faults laid at its door, but this must be the first time that it has been denounced as an attempt at law and order. Citizen Donald seems to have been nearer the mark, from the Anarchist point of view. What the Commune wanted, he opined, was not less law and order, but more — in the shape of drill. (18 March 1887)

[141] Morris had been reluctant to speak in the first place, as he wrote to Jenny on 17 March:

> Today, this evening rather, is our meeting to celebrate the Commune; and I have to speak, which I don't quite like; because although it is proper and right to celebrate the day, one has by this time said all one has to say on the subject. (BL Add. MS. 45, 339; Kelvin 2:627-28)

Coach House, Morris home, 26 Upper Mall, Hammersmith
(Courtesy of the William Morris Gallery)

matter. I hear that the SDF rather paid for *their* egotism by the way; couldn't get the big hall they boasted about, and so were out of it, and had to put up with holding small local meetings.

Sunday the annual meeting of our Hammersmith Branch came off: a dead failure, as all our meetings except the open air ones have been lately.[142] However I really think the savage second winter has had something to do with it; we have had a hard frost for nearly a fortnight now, and often a bitter blast of the NE with it; and our stable meeting room is not very warmable under such conditions.[143]

I lectured in the Chiswick Hall Club and had a scanty audience *and* a dull. It was a new lecture, and good, though I say it,[144] and I really did my best; but they hung on my hands as heavy as lead. The open-air

---

[142] The Branch didn't send a report of its meeting to *Commonweal*, but the issue of 26 March noted, p. 104, 'Celebrations took place at many of the Branches of the Socialist League… .'

[143] Once a coach house, this extension to Morris's London home was earlier used by Morris for weaving, and now served as the Hammersmith Socialist League meeting place.

[144] 'Monopoly', LeMire Cal., p. 262.

meeting at Walham Green in the morning was very creditable considering the cold weather and the underfoot misery.

Thursday 24ᵗʰ — fifty-three years old today — no use grumbling at that. The frost broke on Monday–Tuesday and we have now got reasonable weather. Monday afternoon Mahon called from Newcastle where he has been carrying on a campaign chiefly amongst the miners on strike: he reports well of it:[145] only as he had to work with J. Williams and Hunter Watts (of the SDF) he will hardly be able to form a branch of the League, and thinks that he had better invite them to form a separate body independent of League and SDF: this is awkward but perhaps can't be helped.[146]

Council-meeting short and confused: the two parties rather bitter but not inclined to do much since the Conference comes off so soon: settled now for Whitsunday. Lane gave notice of resolution for next Monday pledging the Council to leave the whole matter of tactics alone at present: I shall support that.[147] I am certainly feeling discouraged about the League: between them they will break it up I fear, and then the SDF will

---

[145] In the 26 March *Commonweal* Mahon published an enthusiastic report, 'The Miners' Strike in Northumberland', signed Newcastle, 22 March.

[146] This was the first sign of what would become, after the 1887 Conference, Mahon's organisation of a North of England Socialist Federation, independent of both SL and SDF. It was based on the SL constitution except for the advocacy of participation in parliamentary campaigns. (Thompson, p. 464)

[147] On 5 May, Morris wrote to Lane outlining his proposed motion(s):

This Conference endorses the past policy of the League in abstaining from parliamentary agitation and the advocacy of merely ameliorative measures,* and it believes that the policy of abstention should be steadily adhered to.

* (or, sees no reason for changing that policy) (Morris's note)

The letter continues, 'I conclude that you would vote for that if your hotter one were lost.' In a postscript he adds,

If that were lost I should move:

That it would be useless and mischievous to put forward a programme advocating an agitation for passing a series of mere ameliorative measures as we believe that such measures would not prove a solution of the struggle between labour and capital and would tend to hinder the progress of the Social Revolution. (BL Add. MS. 46,345)

be the only practical body here; which I don't like the idea of as its advertising tactics make it somewhat ridiculous. I shall move at the conference that the question of parliament or non-parliament be deferred for a year. The Fabians by the way have issued their parliamentary League manifesto:[148] I don't mind this if they like to try it. But the S[ocialist] L[eague] going parliamentary would be a misfortune.[149]

Tuesday 22nd. I gave my 'Feudal England' at Hammersmith Radical Club:[150] nine people for audience! The fact is this is a slack time for lectures.

March 30th, Wednesday. On Sunday I gave my 'Monopoly' at the Borough of Hackney Club, which was one of the first workmen's clubs founded, if not the first;[151] it is a big club numbering 1,600 members: a

---

[148] Under the leadership of Annie Besant, the Fabians made an effort to form a Fabian Parliamentary League in 1887, but they did not begin serious campaigning for another couple of years. See Paul Thompson, *Socialists, Liberals, and Labour: The Struggle for London 1885–1914*, London 1967, pp. 139-40.

[149] After the defeat of Lane's motion Morris elaborated on these views in a letter to Lane of 30 March:

> I think it may at some future time be necessary to send men to parliament as rebels to it: but it is not necessary to educate people towards that, because by that time we shall be strong enough in numbers to send them with no great preparation: therefore we need say nothing about it now. Meanwhile I believe all palliative measures like the 8 hours bill to be delusive, and so, damaging to the cause *if put forward by socialists as a part of socialism*: though of course they will be put forward and carried at some time by some party, and we shall then have to take the good and the bad of them. But we should be clear *that they are not our measures*. I think the duty of the League is educational entirely at present; and that duty is all the more important since the SDF has entirely given up that side of things. (BL Add. MS. 46,345; Kelvin 2:631)

> Underlying Morris's insistent anti-parliamentarianism is his conviction that political campaigns serve no such educational purpose.

[150] On King Street, see Le Mire, Cal., p. 262.

[151] 27 Haggerstone Rd, London, in Stan Shipley, *Club Life and Socialism in Mid-Victorian London*, Journeyman/LHWC, 1983, p. 78.

dirty wretched place enough giving a sad idea of the artisans' standard of comfort: the meeting was a full one, and I suppose I must say attentive; but the coming and going all the time, the pie-boy and the pot-boy was rather trying to my nerves: the audience was civil and inclined to agree, but I couldn't flatter myself that they mostly understood me, simple as the lecture was. This was a morning lecture over about two o'clock: I went afterwards with poor Vandenhout[152] to the Hackney Branch as I had to speak at the 'free-speech demonstration' in Victoria Park. Dined on the way off three pence worth of shrimps that I bought in a shop, and ate with bread and butter and ginger beer in a coffee shop, not as dirty as it looked from outside.

I went afterwards to the Demonstration on Free Speech in Victoria Park:[153] as a demonstration it was a failure, I suppose enough fuss hadn't

---

[152] Vandenhout is a misspelling for Vanderhout. The *West Central News* for 15 December 1877 reports a 'VanderHout' present at an International Labour Union Meeting; a 'Mr Banderhout' attended a Mile End Labour Emancipation League (LEL) meeting to protest Bradlaugh's exclusion from parliament; and *Justice* lists T. Vanderhout as a LEL speaker on 'Freedom in England' and 'Socialism' at Mile End Waste and Gibraltar Walk, Bethnal Green Road in 1884. At a 21 September 1885 SL meeting to protest the Dod St. arrests, a Vanderhout was listed present. The *East London Observer* of 29 August 1885 notes Vanderhout's statement at a Whitechapel suffrage meeting, and, on 14 August 1886, his speech in favour of a local board candidate. In 1886 *Commonweal* listed Vanderhout as speaking on 12 June for the Mile End Branch on the Waste, and the 9 September *Commonweal* reported of a Mile End Branch meeting: 'Van de Hout, who acted as chairman, exposed the capitalistic cry of "foreigners," which socialist are so often met with'. In the November 1888 *East London Observer* J. S. Vanderhout was mentioned as participating in a fight between tailors and masters who were attempting to break up a meeting over sweating (I am indebted for these references to Stan Shipley). J. S. Vanderhout is also the same person as I. S. Van der Hout, who played an important part in the First International in Amsterdam (1872). The adjective 'poor' may be clarified by a letter of 4 February 1887 from Van der Hout in the Amsterdam IISH archives, which states that he is leaving to attend the funeral of his mother; after a visit to the continent to bury his parent he may have been lonely and depressed.

[153] The Free Speech Demonstration was held at 3.30 p.m. in Victoria Park, under the auspices of the Hackney Branch SL, to celebrate the release of James Allman, who was one of their members. *The Times* included no notice; the *Daily News* mentioned it on 29 March under the heading 'Political Meetings'

been made about it: but it was a good Sunday afternoon gathering the crowd very quiet and attentive 300 or 400 I should suppose. Faulkner lectured here in the evening, a good lecture to a better audience than lately.[154] Good meeting at Walham Green: none because of rain at Beadon R[oa]d. Monday's Council meeting was unsatisfactory: Lane brought forward his motion that all members of Council should drop the question of parliamentary agitation; but of course the other side would not agree, and Lane withdrew his motion: he had not quite made it clear that he meant it for a compromise.[155] Donald admitted that some compromise might have to be come to at the Conference. By the way, I forgot to mention that on Monday 27th we discussed at the Branch a motion that I put forward to be moved by the Branch at the Conference, shelving the question for a year; Bolas objected to some of the wording of it, which seemed to him to express opinion as to the matter itself;[156] but did not object to the shelving. Doubtless the Branch will pass it thus amended unanimously. Whatever happens, I fear however that as an organisation we shall come to nothing, though personal feeling may hold us together.

At Monday's meeting Mainwaring brought up a co-operative scheme, the profits made to go to the funds of the League; I rather agree to this

(p. 3); H. A. Barker's notice in the 2 April *Commonweal* reported speeches by Morris, Scheu, Sparling, Barker, Mainwaring, Lane, Davis, and James Allman, and passage of a motion protesting police interference: 'The meeting throughout was enthusiastic, and cheers of welcome were given our comrade Allman.' (p. 111)

[154] *Commonweal* announced C.J. Faulkner's 27 March talk on 'Inhuman Arithmetic', and Faulkner published an article in *Commonweal* under the same title in two installments on 30 July and 6 August 1887.

[155] Morris's letter of 30 March to Lane comments on the resolution's purpose as a compromise:

Of course I consider the resolution to shelve the question (ie, to shelve the definite conclusion on it, for whatever happens it will certainly be talked about), as a compromise, which would allow latitude of opinion while it lasted. I hate compromises personally; but do not see how one is to be avoided at this crisis if the League is to go on and the *Commonweal* also. (BL Add. MS. 46,345; Kelvin 2:632)

[156] Tom Bolas was a member both of the Hammersmith Branch SL and of the Fabian Society, for whom he had edited the *Practical Socialist* in 1886. Since the Fabians had just adopted their Parliamentary Manifesto, perhaps he wanted to remain at least neutral on the issue.

so as to give our people something to do; though of course I see its disadvantages.[157]

Thursday 31st. Yesterday I got a letter from Lane about his canvassing the Branches on the anti-parliamentary side;[158] I am afraid he won't do much good if he goes, though his obvious earnestness and good faith make him a convincing speaker. I also wrote to Maguire of the Leeds Branch urging him to adopt the compromise: Lane says he will accept that. Charles called to say goodbye: he is broke here and is going to America.[159] They are at it in the House about the Coercion Bill, which

---

[157] The 23 April 1887 *Commonweal* announced the formation of a Co-operative Store at the SL office, to sell groceries Mondays, Wednesdays, and Saturdays after 8.30 p.m.; the last advertisement appeared on 16 July of the same year. Morris's objections would probably have been to the limited and palliative nature of co-operative merchandising as a cure for the injustices of capitalism; of course his limited agreement on the grounds that it would 'give our people something to do' might have applied equally well to limited electoral campaigns.

[158] Morris wrote to Lane the day he received his letter, urging him not to give up his employment and offering £5 to aid with expenses. In a portion of the letter marked 'private again', he promised, 'I am writing today to Maguire of the Leeds Branch to urge him and his branch to adopt the Compromise.' (BL Add. MS. 46,345; Kelvin 2:632)

[159] A member of the North London branch and SL council member for its first two years, Henry Charles became the *Commonweal* American correspondent, sending news of the Haymarket trials later in the year. Morris wrote him a letter dated 16 June [1887] describing the conference and new council members, and adding:

> … meantime you can be comforted by thinking that we miss you, as we do very much.

His tone is one of speaking to an ally and fellow-anti-parliamentarian:

> … the upshot is that we are very weak, and our work is increased very much, and not to croak, I fear it will be difficult to hold the League together even if the others don't capture it, which of course they will try to do.

In view of Quail's mention of Charles' later anarchist activities, it is interesting that Morris comments on anarchism to Charles as follows:

> As to Anarchism, I am not an Anarchist as I understand the word, though I dislike the pedantry of the Collectivist leaders. (autograph, Houghton Library; Kelvin 2:668-69)

Charles seems to have remained in the U.S. until his death in 1926 (see biographical note).

will however be carried, I suppose, as the Tory and Whig majority is overwhelming. If only the radicals would exert themselves and come out into the streets and make a great show, which they might do,[160] the Whigs and Liberal Unionists might be frightened into voting against it; but I can't see that there is any enthusiasm against it outside the mere party business.

April 27th. I have been busy about many things and so unable to fill up this book. I have had a propaganda tour in the north of which I now give some account. I got to Glasgow in the morning of April 3rd and was met by Muirhead Glasier, and other members of the branch: I spoke at a meeting, their ordinary Sunday one, on the Green; the audience something like our London ones but I should say more intelligent, knew better what was being spoken about, I mean.[161]

In the evening I lectured in the Waterloo Hall to a big audience, say 1,000:[162] which was good as they had to pay. Cunninghame Graham MP

---

[160] Two weeks later the radicals did just that, gathering 100,000 people in Hyde Park to protest the Coercion bill; see Morris's 27 April entry. In every April issue *Cw*'s front page news featured a discussion of legislation on Ireland.

[161] In order to arrive in time, Morris had taken the night train; he wrote to May on 4 April:

> I had a very comfortable journey down in a coupé 2/6 to the guard ensured my sole holding of it; and my supper was splendid. The morning was beautiful and dawn broke before we got to Shap [Cumbria], so I had a good view of the mountains. (Henderson, *Letters*, p. 268; Kelvin 2:637)

Of the open-air meeting at 1 p.m., Morris wrote to Jenny on 14 April:
> Well I began operations by helping the ordinary open-air meeting in Jail Square (ominous name) which is just in front of a doleful openish garden called the Green: a meeting much like ours in London a good one of its kind… (*Letters*, p. 269; Kelvin 2:641)

The Glasgow branch report to *Commonweal* notes:
> After Glasier had spoken, comrade William Morris addressed the meeting, his concise and vigorous statement of the labour question being listened to with great attention and sympathy by the audience. (9 April, p. 120)

[162] His subject was 'True and False Society', a lecture which he gave several times in 1886 and 1887; see Le Mire Cal., p. 262 and Checklist, no. 90 p. 307. The April *Commonweal* branch report emphasises the uniqueness of Cunninghame-Graham's presence:

took the chair for me, which was thought bold on a Sunday and a Socialist meeting: he declared himself not a socialist because he agreed with the Owenite doctrine of man being made by his circumstances; which seemed strange, and I rather took him up on that point. The lecture was well received, and a Socialist resolution carried. The next day I went to Dundee, to a certain parson David Macrea, once a U[nited] P[resbytarian] minister but turned out for heresy, and now running a congregation on his own hook. My position was only to form part of the fortnightly entertainment which he gives to his flock, music and a terrible recitation being the bulk of it as to time: however I spoke for forty minutes (from notes) and got a good deal into the space: the audience was large, 'respectable', mostly lower middle class, and seemed rather startled, but not unfriendly.[163] I went to Edinburgh next day and lectured in that hall again:[164] audience small, my last lecture had discounted this I doubt: old Bone was tiresome, the chairman, a very good fellow was not a good chairman; but we carried our resolution, though clearly there were many dissentients at one time in the hall: those who agreed seemed very hearty. Slept at Glasse's. The next day went to Glasgow again,[165] and met the Branch and friends at a tea-party, which was rather a slow affair: there I got a letter from London urging me to go to help Mahon in the

---

The meeting was a unique one. For the first time in the history of Scotland a Scottish MP took part in a political meeting held on a Sunday, and for the first time in the history of Britain a British MP presided at a Socialist meeting. Although disclaiming the title of a Socialist, Cunninghame-Graham expressed himself deeply in sympathy with the aims of Socialists. (p. 120)

[163] No newspaper was published in Dundee in 1887 in which to search for references to this meeting. Morris noted to May, 'Dundee a good audience as to number but not the right thing.' (*Letters*, p. 268)

[164] The trip from Dundee to Edinburgh had stirred memories; Morris wrote to Jenny, 'You know one has about 20 minutes sea from Fife across the firth to Granton, whence of old times I set sail to Iceland.' (Henderson, *Letters*, p. 270; Kelvin 2:641)

[165] En route to Glasgow Morris had stopped to see a palace and church at Linlithgow, noting distastefully the 'feeble attempt at restoration'. (Henderson, *Letters*, p. 270; Kelvin 2:642) The 16 April *Commonweal* reported cheerfully of the tea:

Over fifty persons were present. After tea Morris read the speech of John Ball, after which the evening was spent in songs, recitations, and speeches. (p. 125)

Newcastle district on Easter Monday;[166] so, much against my will I wired him that I would do so. The next day we went to Hamilton which is the centre of the coal mining district: the miners had gone in on a sort of compromise, but were beaten in point of fact: so it is hardly to be wondered at that this was a depressing affair: we met in an inn parlour some members of the Branch which seems to be moribund, and they would scarcely say a word and seemed in last depths of depression: the hall, not a large one, was nothing like full; it was a matter of course that there was no dissent, but there was rather a chilly feeling over all.[167] A comic event enlivened us of a drunken man in the gallery who insisted on mistaking me for his representative Mr Mason,[168] and quarrelling with me on some political matter which the liquor told him I was saying.

Paisley was the next place: nor was this a very lively meeting, chiefly I think because our Glasgow friends had not had time or opportunity

---

To Jenny, Morris noted that the party was 'rather slow; our Scotch friends not being very good at that sort of thing they are so shy.' (Henderson, *Letters*, p. 270; Kelvin 2:642)

[166] This was to be an 11 April meeting in support of the striking miners; see note 182 below. Morris had complained to May:

> ... here's a go!
>
> I have been so bullied to go to Newcastle and speak at the miners' meeting so as not to let the SDF reap where we have sowed that I have given way and shall speak there on Monday... I don't like the job but it all comes in the day's work.... (6 April, Henderson, *Letters*, p. 268; Kelvin 2:639)

[167] Choral Hall, John McMunn presiding. *Commonweal* observed:

> The meeting was not so large as was expected, owing probably to the miners being so much dispirited with the result of their recent strike. Those present, however, were entirely sympathetic, and a resolution in favour of Socialism, moved and seconded by the Secretary and President of the Hamilton miners, was carried unanimously. (16 April)

The *Hamilton Advertiser* gave laconic and obscure coverage at the bottom of p. 6 col.2:

> The lecturer received a patient hearing, but after he sat down the limited audience thinned somewhat, the invitation given to ask questions not being sufficient to induce them to stay. Some amusement was caused by the style in which a gentleman in the gallery argued with Mr Morris.

[168] Stephen Mason was a Gladstonian Liberal MP for Mid-Lanarkshire from 1881–88.

to work it up: once more there was no dissent.[169] The Provost (Mayor Anglic[is]e) took the chair a curious old body once a chartist I think.[170] The next day Saturday we went to Coatbridge the centre of the iron district and held an open air meeting at a sort of open space by a canal at the end of that miserable cinder heap, lighted up, as night came on cold and clear, with the flare of the iron furnaces.[171] We were late as we did not get out at the proper station; so we had to compete with a cheap-jack and the Salvation Army, but had a pretty good meeting too; only disturbed by a drunken Irishman.[172]

---

[169] In Good Templars' Hall, Paisley, he spoke on 'Socialism: the Way and the Means', see Le Mire Cal., p. 263 and Le Mire Ch., no. 94 p. 308. Morris had first delivered this talk the preceding fall, and gave it twelve times between September 1886 and April 1887. The *Radical Times* of Paisley, which had just begun with its 19 February 1887 issue, published an enthusiastic article on 2 April heralding Morris's visit:

> Unlike many critics he does not confine his ideas to mere theory, but has set about showing by his own handicraft what art in application to decoration should be. (p. 7 col. 3)

The 9 April issue, its last, contains no reference to Morris's speech of 8 April. The *Radical Times*' short lifespan seems to have followed the fortunes of the strike. The *Paisley Gazette* gave no coverage; Le Mire cites a report which I have been unable to locate in the *Paisley Daily Express*. (9 April, p. 3)

[170] Robert Cochrane, Provost of Paisley from 1885–88, was born in 1808, at the time of the *Diary* was seventy-nine years old, and lived until 1897. A former weaver and chartist, Cochrane helped organise the reform procession of 9 May 1831, and was for many years Honorary President of the Paisley Liberal Club; he considered himself a lifelong radical, and attempted unsuccessfully to become a Liberal parliamentary candidate in 1880. He held local governmental positions from 1864–96, serving as ward representative, magistrate, Justice of the Peace, and Provost. His obituary described him as familiar with Scottish poetry, a good conversationalist, and possessed of 'a rare fund of reminiscence and anecdote'. (*Paisley and Renfrewshire Gazette*, 26 June 1897; source, Daniel Cameron, Librarian, Local History Dept.)

[171] The Cross, Coatbridge, see Le Mire Cal., p. 263. The *Coatbridge Express* declined to comment on Morris's visit, and remarked under 'Local Topics':

> This week the uppermost topic in Coatbridge has of course been the appearance, or perhaps the reappearance of the Choral Union of the burgh in a grand choral and orchestral interpretation of Handel's 'Messiah'…. (13 April, p. 2 col.1)

The same issue reported the death of a miner in a pit accident, his body mutilated almost beyond recognition. (p. 1 col.3)

The next day Sunday I spoke to quite a big meeting on the Green[173] before leaving for Newcastle where a socialist and anticoercion resolution (one of each) was passed. The audience quite enthusiastic. The Glasgow Branch is in good condition apparently are working hard, and getting a good deal of support. There are some very nice fellows amongst them; they are a good deal made up of clerks designers and the like, and rather under the thumbs of their employers or they would be able to do more. Kropotkin's visit has turned them a little in the Anarchist direction, which gives them an agreeable air of toleration, and they are at present quite innocent of any parliamentary designs.[174] The feeling amongst the working men about is certainly in favour of Socialism; but they are slack in joining any organisation as usual: still the thing is taking hold.

Sunday evening I went to Newcastle and was received by Donald and Mahon, and presently stumbled on Hyndman who had been lecturing that evening.[175] I was pressed to come down to Newcastle because the SDF after seeming to agree that neither organisation should press itself on the miners has been playing a double game and trying to bag them

---

[172] Morris gave more details in his 14 April letter to Jenny:

There we... had a good meeting only disturbed by a drunken Irish man, who insisted with many oaths on our telling him the difference between a Home-Ruler and a non-Home-Ruler, and swore by Christ that he would teach us Socialism he would: but the crowd soon put him down. All this we did by star and furnace light, which was strange and even dreadful. (Henderson, *Letters*, p. 271; Kelvin 2:642)

Commonweal euphemised the 'Irish drunk':

Some objections were offered in a very fair spirit by one of the audience, to which Morris replied. (16 April, p. 125)

[173] *Commonweal* estimated the Glasgow Green crowd at 1,000 to 1,200 (16 April), and Morris described them to Jenny as 'a large audience on the Green who were very sympathetic; but sadly poor and pinched they look as they well may'. (Henderson, *Letters*, p. 271; Kelvin 2:642-43)

[174] Kropotkin had visited Glasgow in 1886, speaking under SL auspices on 27 November on the topic, 'Socialism: Its Growing Force and Final Aim'. Woodcock and Avakomovic (*The Anarchist Prince*, London 1950, p. 213) list another trip in the early spring of 1887, but do not give a date; neither *Commonweal* nor *Freedom* make mention of it.

[175] Surprisingly the 9 and 16 April issues of *Justice* omit mention of Hyndman's tour.

after all. Well, next morning we started for the collieries early, and came to a place called Seghill,[176] where went into a miner's cottage and D[onald] and I sat down and talked while Mahon went to arrange matters, as there was to be a converging march on the field at Horton where the meeting was to be. The goodman was a tall strong man his face wrecked by an accident which had blown out one eye and damaged the other: he seemed a kindly intelligent man, and gave us all information carefully, speaking without any bitterness against the masters: the strike is on this wise; the men were working about four days a week and only earning after all deductions about thirteen s[hillings], and the masters are for reducing their wages by twelve and a half per cent on the grounds that the price of coal justifies this reduction, although according to the sliding scale of wages agreed to by employers and employed this was not called for: so the miners are striking against this reduction. The man's wife and daughter were about, tidy and good-tempered women, his house was very clean as clean as a cottage in the country, and so were apparently most of the others inside,[177] though they are most woeful looking dwellings of man, and the whole district is just a miserable back yard to the collieries. Mahon and I leaving D[onald] behind went by train to Blyth (which is a seaport)[178] and at the station found a considerable crowd waiting for us who followed us into the market place where I spoke to them from a trolley for about forty minutes while Mahon again saw to some business. Then we started without any show or banners or band, and consequently without many

---

[176] The bleakness of the collieries had impressed Morris:

Early the next morning we started off for the collieries, and alighted from the train in a wretched-looking country enough; not smoky, for alack the collieries are not working, but so waste and desolate looking like — well 'a back yard' on a large scale. The roads of course were black…. (Henderson, *Letters*, p. 271; Kelvin 2:643)

Seghill is seven miles northeast of Newcastle-upon-Tyne, and Morris described it to Jenny as a collection of pitmen's houses. (Henderson, *Letters*, p. 272; Kelvin 2:646)

[177] Characteristically Morris commented on the interior arrangement of the houses:

… most of them as we passed their open door showed a swell but ugly bedstead in the place of honour… (Henderson, *Letters*, p. 272; Kelvin 2:647)

[178] Misspelt by Morris as Blithe, this is about thirteen miles northeast of Newcastle on the sea.

with us:[179] about halfway however we picked up a band and a banner and a lot of men, and soon swelled into a respectable company: the others had got there before us and lots more were streaming up into the field: the day was bright and sunny, the bright blue sea forming a strange border to the misery of the land.[180] We spoke from one waggon Fielding of the SDF in the chair,[181] then Mahon then me then Hyndman then Donald. It was a very good meeting: the front ranks sat down to let the others hear and see. The audience listened intently and were heartily with us: they began by objecting to the reporters, and cried out to 'put them out' unless they put all down. They hooted the police lustily when I said something about those worthies;[182] being much excited by the news of J. Williams' arrest in London the day before, as he has been down speaking to them.[183] I note that my speech as given in the

---

[179] To Jenny he described the crowd at first as 'rather a draggle-tailed lot'. (Henderson, *Letters*, p. 272; Kelvin 2:647)

[180] The contrast between sea and land had impressed him, as he recalled:
> Blithe is a sea-port, and as we came in I could see the masts of ships there: and as we plodded on through the dreary (O so dreary) villages, & that terrible waste of the endless back-yard, we could see on our left hand a strip of the bright blue sea, for it was a beautiful sunny day. (Henderson, *Letters*, p. 272; Kelvin 2:647)

[181] This was John Fielding, ardent recruiter for the SDF, of whom *Justice* remarked in its report on the meeting:
> A great work has been done here and John Fielding deserves the highest credit for the determination and vigour which he has displayed under the most difficult circumstances. Branches of the Social-Democratic Federation are being formed under his auspices not only in Newcastle itself, but in all the mining villages round…. (16 April, p. 1 col. 2)

[182] Morris had asserted,
> Even these men that were dressed in blue with bright buttons upon them and white gloves (Voices: 'Out with them') — and those other men dressed in red, and also sometimes with gloves on their fingers, what were they: Simply working men, very hard up, driven into a corner and compelled to put on the livery of a set of masters. (Hear, hear, and prolonged hooting.) (*Newcastle Chronicle*, 12 April, p. 4)

[183] John Williams of the SDF had spoken to Newcastle miners at a gathering on 6 April; four days later, on 10 April, he was arrested and charged with 'riotous conduct' for speaking and selling *Justice* in a Hyde Park Sunday afternoon meeting.

Chronicle is verbatim almost; as I fancy is Hyndman's, but Donald I thought made the speech of the occasion.[184] We three hurried off to catch the train for Newcastle which we just did, and got hungry but passed there in time [to] have a bite and drop in the refreshment rooms. There Joseph Cowen stumbled on us and we had a friendly talk together[185] and

---

[184] Morris inserted the *Newcastle Chronicle* 12 April account into the *Diary* facing pp. 44 and 45; the report gives almost eighteen inches of coverage of Morris's speech and more than twenty inches to Hyndman's, but dismisses Donald in two inches. Morris's speech described the capitalistic system as war and warned that under capitalism one local strike would only lead to another; instead he advocated a general workingmen's strike:

> He believed that that crisis would take the form, after they had made those claims which they would have to make, of the entire, complete, and immediate submission of their masters. (*Newcastle Chronicle*, 12 April, p. 4)

The demonstration was sufficiently large to receive modest coverage in the London press; on 12 April brief articles appeared in *The Times* (p. 8 col.5), *Pall Mall Gazette* (p. 10 col. 2), *Daily News* (p. 6 col. 4), and the *Daily Standard* (p. 3 col. 6); all but the *Pall Mall Gazette* mentioned Morris.

[185] Joseph Cowen, the former Radical MP from Newcastle, had retired from Parliament the preceding year. Cowen had been briefly associated with Hyndman and paid the latter's bail when several members of the SDF were arrested on 8 February 1886. Morris had invited him to contribute to *Commonweal*, and in Cowen's answer of 15 November 1886, he declared his clear divergence from the Socialists:

> … the paper you speak of, the *Commonweal*, I don't remember to have seen. I feel myself in a somewhat peculiar position with respect to your request. I am not a socialist and never was. All my inclinations and convictions are the other way. I have been, for many years, on friendly terms with most of the leading English and Continental Socialists, and when they have been claiming the right to be heard, I have been on their side. But I have never been able to see my way to assist in propagating their views. [I have helped Hyndman] with *Justice* more with the view of encouraging workmen to undertake the printing and publishing of a paper of their own, than out of sympathy with the doctrines they proclaim. (BL Add. MS. 45,345)

After the firmness of the letter, Cowen's cordiality may have been a mild surprise; Morris's description of the event to Jenny emphasises his friendliness:

> … who should come up but Joseph Cowen very friendly and nice, I must say, and we had a talk, all we could in twenty minutes space. (Henderson, *Letters*, p. 273; Kelvin 2:648)

saw us off by train to a place called Ryton Willows where we had advertised another meeting: it is a piece of rough healthy ground by the Tyneside under the bank by which the railway runs: it is a pretty place and the evening was lovely: a mere recreation ground with swings and merry-go-rounds.[186] But we had a very fair meeting there of most attentive persons, though I guess I tried their patience as I got 'lectury' and being excited went on and on till I had gone on too long: however it was successful and the audience stayed till it was nearly dark, gave three cheers for the Socialists and off we went back.[187]

The next day I went up to London and got to the Council in time to come in for one of the usual silly squabbles about nothing,[188] and to propose a Hyde Park meeting in aid of the Northumbrian miners in a fortnight which was agreed to.[189] There is no doubt of the success (which may be temporary) which we have made in these northern mining districts.

I spoke the next Sunday at Beadon Road and couldn't help contrasting our cockneys much to their disadvantage with the northerners: the meeting fair, also a good one at Walham Green, and at our room in the evening where I lectured. The Easter Monday anticoercion meeting was

---

[186] Morris had at first questioned the suitability of the location:
> … it is a recreation ground and being Easter Monday there were lots of folk there with swings and cricket and dancing and the like: I thought it a queer place for a serious Socialist meeting… .
> (Henderson, *Letters*, p. 273; Kelvin 2:648)

[187] His private description reiterates the sense of fellowship which the meeting inspired:
> … we had a crowd about us in no time and I spoke, rather too long I fancy, till the stars came out and it grew dusk and the people stood & listened still, & when we were done they gave three cheers for the Socialists, & all was mighty friendly & pleasant: & so back we went to supper and bed, of which I for one was glad enough.
> (Henderson, *Letters*, p. 273; Kelvin 2:648)

[188] Compare Morris's wryly dispassionate interpretation later in the summer:
> It is so bewilderingly irritating to see perfectly honest men, very enthusiastic, and not at all self-seeking, and less stupid than most people, squabble so: and withal for the most part they are personally good friends together. (Mackail, vol. II, pp. 184-85)

[189] The meeting was held 24 April; see note 191. For a criticism of the SL's failure to grasp the political implications of the miners' strike and its defeat, see Thompson, p. 438.

certainly a success;[190] I have no doubt much bigger than the Suffrage-meeting where we got hustled three years ago.[191] The democratic element was dominant in it, and the socialists very popular.

The next Monday meeting at Farringdon R[oa]d was the meeting of London members also, and Lane read his manifesto; which indeed turned out to be a long lecture not at all fit for its purpose, and which would have been damaging to us antiparliamentarians if it had gone to the Branches:[192] a vote was taken as to whether the Council should be advised to print it and the majority report and it was carried that it should not be, I voted in the majority.

The next Sunday 24th our Hyde Park meeting came off on a stormy day, but was a fair success under the circumstances, although a hail storm drove a lot of people out of the Park just as we were beginning.[193] Note that all this time anticoercion meetings are being held all about:

---

[190] For reports of the enormous 11 April Hyde Park Anti-Coercion meeting, see 12 April, *The Times* (p. 9 cols 4-6) and *Daily News* (p. 6 cols 3 and 4); the former estimated an attendance of 40,000-50,000; the latter reported 150,000, and described in addition the demonstrations of the SL and SDF. The 16 April *Commonweal* was of course pleased:

> We have said that it was the largest ever held there, but this conveys no clear idea of its gigantic size; the reports of the bourgeois press of course vary and contradict one another in their usual stupid fashion, but even from them it is clear that over 150,000, probably near 200,000, persons were present in support of the meeting; while the lookers-on, all of whom seemed in sympathy, were quite beyond all hope of computation. (p. 124)

A similar Anti-Coercion and Unemployed meeting the following 13 November would become Bloody Sunday, at which police charged protestors and bystanders, resulting in approximately 200 people treated for injuries and three deaths. (Thompson, p. 491; reports vary)

[191] Morris refers to the attack on socialist speakers by a Radical working men's crowd which had gathered on 23 July 1884 to protest the rejection of the Third Reform Act (County Franchise) by the House of Lords. (see Kelvin 2:309-10, July 26)

[192] In November 1886, the SL Council appointed a committee of Bax, Binning, Mahon, and Lane to draft a policy statement for the 1887 conference; the other three favoured a parliamentary position, but Lane wrote a minority report. Morris had previously discouraged him from printing his manifesto for circulation to the branches before the Conference, and had argued against the use of the term anti-statist. (30 March and 16 May, BL Add. MS. 46,345; Kelvin 2:631 and 651)

but to my thinking there is no great enthusiasm about it except among regular political persons.[194] Still it is something that the political Democracy has taken it up.

By the by on Sunday 24th Brocher came to lecture here about Colins the Belgian Utopist Socialist and had no audience:[195] he is not in any case a lively lecturer though an interesting man and also the Hyde Park meeting damaged us no doubt: still it was discouraging. Council meeting on Monday 25th. Lane and Mainwaring very much in opposition and not a little unreasonable: a kind of discussion as to the 'making of a Conference being made' like the gate of the old Medieval King. Donald practically sent to Northumberland to help to resist the intrigues of the SDF. The papers full during these days of the Snabele arrest;[196] my private opinion is — war.[197]

---

[193] In its 30 April issue (p. 137 col. 2), *Commonweal* printed an abridged report from the surprisingly sympathetic *London Daily Chronicle*:

> The proceedings throughout were most orderly, and the attendance of about 40 or 45 constables, who stood in couples on the fringe of the gathering, seemed somewhat unnecessary.

Morris had moved a resolution, and his speech was well-reported (p. 138):

> This strike was simply one of the incidents in the great warfare of labour against capital, which the present system rendered it imperative for the working men to carry on… As long as there were employers and employed there would be war between them… The miners of the North were beginning to look at the matter from the Socialists' point of view, and as soon as the workers clearly understood that they must have their destiny in their own hands it would not be difficult to get rid of the present system.

Donald, Kitz, Wardle, and Mainwaring also made speeches.

[194] In the 23 April *Commonweal*, Morris expressed similar doubts about the efficacy of anti-coercion agitation:

> The popular opposition, respectable as it is, does not seem to be of that volume and energy which implies a threat of consequences beyond the ballot-box; and as to the vote, the agitation is discounted by the Tories because they know that a very large proportion of the agitators have not got it…. (p. 132)

[195] See note 115; as announced in the 23 April *Commonweal*, Brocher's talk was scheduled for 8 p.m. on 'Colins and his Philosophical and Social System'. See Colins biographical entry.

[196] According to the 22 April *Daily News*, Monsieur Schnaebell, the special French Commissary at the Railway Station at Pagny-sur-Moselle, had been

List of Newspaper Clippings Inserted by Morris in the *Socialist Diary*

1. Within entry for 25 January: 'The Disturbances at Norwich', letter from William Morris to the editor of *The Daily News*.

2. Within entry for 12 February: report 'The Socialist Demonstration in Clerkenwell / The Siege of a Butcher's Shop', *The Daily News*, 10 February 1887.

3. Within entry for 23 February: 'Against (ii.) By Mr W Morris', article labelled by Morris, 'a railway proposed from Windermere to Ambleside intending to go right through the Lake Country in time / *Pall Mall Gazette*, 22 February 1887.'

4. Within entry for 21 March: report 'Celebrating the Commune', *The Daily News* Friday, 18 March 1887.

5. Within entry for 21 March: report 'Socialist Meetings in Newcastle. / Speeches by Mr Mahon'. *Newcastle Daily Chronicle* 7 March 1887.

6. Within entry for 21 March: 'Manifesto of the Fabian Parliamentary League'.

7. Within entry for 27 April: report 'The Socialists and the Miners / The Great Demonstration at Horton / Speeches by Messrs Morris and Hyndman', *Newcastle Daily Chronicle* 12 April 1887.

8. Within entry for 27 April: report 'Meeting at Ryton' and 'The Arrest of Mr John Williams', *Newcastle Daily Chronicle* 12 April 1887.

---

arrested by the German Police Commissary of Arts and taken to Metz; a debate ensued over whether he had been arrested on French or German soil. On 23, 25 and 26 April the *Daily News* continued to express worry over the possibility of war. Morris wasn't the only one confused about the spelling of the French Commissary's name; the *Daily News* alternatively spelled it Schnaebell, Schnaebele, and Schnaebel. Excitement abated after the prisoner was released on 29 April.

[197] Compare Morris's final sentiment with the statements of his first entry; as so often, he exaggerated the immediacy of a threat of war. But by later in the year he was more sceptical:

> The new Socialist law is no doubt a sign of progress, and may be a sign of approaching European war, though I decline to be any longer moved by war scares which are probably got up by statesmen-thieves or stockjobbing d[itt]o.... (December 1887, 'The Present Outlook in Politics', LeMire, p. 214)

Biographical Notes

ALLMAN, JAMES, b. 1864/5

Born in Shoreditch, London, Allman was a member of the Mile End branch SL. He was arrested on several occasions for speaking in public; when arrested at Dod Street in 1885, he was listed as a shopman of 5 New North Road, and when arraigned again in 1886, he was described as a tailor's presser. His third arrest in February 1887 is recorded in the *Diary*, and the ensuing report in the *Hackney and Kingsland Gazette* for 23 February describes him as twenty-one years of age, living at Christian Street, Commercial Road, E., and 'a leader among the local socialists'. On each of the three occasions newspaper accounts record his spirited defence to the judge (*Daily News*, 22 September 1885; *East London Observer*, 4 March 1886; see also footnote [92]).

Allman was elected a SL Council member in 1887, and Thompson describes him as unemployed later in the year (Thompson, p. 404), when he worked to organize meetings for the unemployed. *Commonweal* of 11 February lists Allman as one of the speakers at a meeting on Tower Hill. He also played the role of Sergeant Sticktoit in the 1887 Socialist League performance of *The Tables Turned*.

In 1903 and 1906 the Chicago socialist publisher Charles Kerr issued the 113-page *God's Children: A Modern Allegory* by a James Allman, possibly the former SL member. Set in London's East End and presented through the voice of an authoritative socialist speaker, *A Modern Allegory* cites a passage from Morris's 'March of the Workers' as well as lines from Shelley and Kipling.

AVELING, EDWARD, 1849–98, and ELEANOR MARX, 1856–98

A prominent figure in the early socialist movement and an amateur dramatist, Edward Aveling had earned a doctorate in zoology before beginning a career as a secularist and later as a socialist lecturer and journalist. Although Aveling was respected for his abilities, his evasive financial and sexual behaviour embarrassed and angered fellow socialists. During his fifteen-year union with Eleanor Marx, the ardently socialist youngest daughter of Karl Marx, the Avelings were vigorous defenders of their cause. They joined the secession from the SDF which formed the SL, but maintained a strong pro-parliamentary stance in the Bloomsbury branch, and promoted its separation in 1888 to form an independent group, later affiliated with the Labour Emancipation

Eleanor Marx Aveling, Wilhelm Liebknecht, and Edward Aveling
(Source: Wiki)

League. Shortly after Aveling had contracted a secret marriage elsewhere, and in a period of exhaustion from nursing him after surgery, Eleanor Marx committed suicide at the age of forty-three, and Aveling died later the same year. Their lives are movingly told in Yvonne Kapp's two-volume *Eleanor Marx* (London 1972 and 1976) and in Rachel Holmes' *Eleanor Marx: A Life* (Bloomsbury Publishing, 2014). Morris disliked Aveling sufficiently to speak of him in a letter to Glasse as 'that disreputable dog Aveling' (23 September 1887, in Kelvin 2:693). Although in 1885 Morris praised one of Eleanor Marx's speeches highly in a letter to May (18 April, cited in Kapp, vol. 2, p. 40), and Kapp claims that 'they worked together in harmony and with mutual respect, even admiration at this period', (p. 43), Morris made few references to Eleanor Marx apart from Aveling, and indicates in the *Diary* that by 1887 he found 'civility' from the Avelings worthy of record. See also footnote [14].

BARKER, HENRY ALFRED, 1858–1940

Born in Shoreditch, Henry Barker completed primary school in Hoxton before beginning work in his father's construction company at age fourteen. From the late 1870s to the early 1890s he attended classes on hygiene at the National Secular Society Hall of Science, obtaining an advanced certificate in hygiene in 1893. Around 1885 he joined the Hoxton Labour Emancipation League, affiliated as the Hoxton branch of the SL, and became its secretary and an active campaigner for free speech, organizing a protest against the arrest of the Haymarket anarchists. Barker frequently wrote branch reports for *Commonweal*; on 16 October 1886 he recorded that he had spoken the previous week on 'Socialism and Dynamite', and he contributed *Commonweal* articles, 'Is the Miners' Union a Failure?' (10 September 1887), 'The Condition of the Working Classes' (3 December 1887), and 'Prisoners for Liberty' (25 February 1888). The 21 January 1888 *Commonweal* reported an SL performance of his extravaganza 'The Lamp', in which he, his sister, brothers, Joseph Lane, and others acted. A parliamentarian (Tsuzuki, *H.M. Hyndman*, p. 85), Barker was a member of the League Council from 1886 to 1888 and served as secretary in 1887–88; Morris wrote to Glasier in August 1888, 'The Sec. is (to speak plainly) a failure as such, though a very good fellow.' (*Letters*, p. 298)

Barker joined J. L. Mahon, A. K. Donald, Thomas Binning and others in forming the Labour Union in 1888, and as its candidate for the first London County Council election in 1889 he polled 169 votes. After organizing a failed 1890 postal strike, the Labour Union lost credibility, but Barker and others joined in the founding of the Independent Labour Party in 1892, and he later helped in organizing the London Congress of the Second International in 1896. From 1894 onwards he was associated with the Brotherhood Church in Southgate Road, Islington. The same year he married Cecily Ruth Manning, who had also obtained a certificate in hygiene from the National Secular Society's Department of Science, and the couple had five children. His entry in the *Dictionary of Labour Biography* notes that he wrote 'much verse', and that next to

115

politics, 'his main intellectual and emotional interest was poetry.' (p. 20)

Barker left behind scattered notes on William Morris, now in the William Morris Gallery (J194), in which he claimed that 'Morris had not what is called the gift of oratory, but he always spoke with feeling often with considerable heat'. Of his speech at the funeral of Alfred Linnell, Barker added, 'There was fearful earnestness in his voice when referring to the victim we had just laid to rest. Morris cried out 'let us feel he is our brother.' The ring of brotherly love in it was most affecting'. (ff. 2-3). For more details, see Barbara Neild and John Saville, 'Henry Alfred Barker,' *Dictionary of Labour Biography*, vol. 6, 1982, 18-21.

BAX, ERNEST BELFORT, 1854-1926

One of the first British Marxist theorists, Bax joined the SDF in 1882. A fierce opponent of Christianity, women's suffrage and the bourgeois family, advocate of a new socialist consciousness, and author of *The*

Ernest Belfort Bax 1916
Courtesy of the National Portrait Gallery

Religion of Socialism (1885), *The Ethics of Socialism* (1887), and several other books, Bax co-edited with J.L. Joynes the socialist monthly *To-day*, 1884-89, and collaborated with Morris in writing the *Commonweal* essays originally titled 'Socialism from the Root Up,' which were republished in 1893 as *Socialism: Its Growth and Outcome.* A parliamentarian of the Croydon Branch, Bax had left the SDF with Morris to found the SL in 1885, but he returned to the SDF in 1888, where he edited *Justice* for a brief period in 1892 and defended internationalism against Hyndman's support of British nationalism. He later followed Hyndman into the National Socialist Party during World War 1 and afterwards back to the SDF, where he remained until his death. In his *Reminiscences and Reflections of a Mid and Late Victorian* (1918), Bax asserted of Morris: 'The foundation of the Socialist League and the work he put into it reflects the highest credit on Morris personally… Altogether a more personally disinterested man in his public work never existed'. (p. 83) See also footnotes [19] and [20].

BEASLEY, ALFRED, 1847–1925

Born in Rugby, Warwickshire, the son of a shoemaker, Beasley moved to London where he married and worked as a railway clerk, settling first in Ealing and then by 1881 in Hammersmith, where he remained until retirement. One of the first members of the Hammersmith Branch SL, Beasley had joined the Democratic Federation in 1884 and listed himself in a July 1884 branch meeting as living at 28 Masborough Road, Brook Green (now Masbro Road, W10, north of Brook Green). In September 1884 he presented a small library of books for a branch library, and served as one of the branch librarians. He was an occasional open-air speaker, mentioned in the Hammersmith Minute Book as speaking at Hyde Park on 25 October 1885, and on 26 July 1885 he lectured to the branch on 'Private Property'. He was a clear dissenter from SDF tactics, speaking in support of a 18 January 1885 motion by John Carruthers in favor of decentralization and separation from the SDF:

> Mr Beasley said that to his knowledge the tone of *Justice* in advocating the physical force of mere undisciplined mobs disgusted many thinking men with the exponents of socialism, and he would support the motion. (Hammersmith Socialist Society Minutes B. L. Add. MS. 45,891)

He died at Hanwell, Middlesex in 1925.

BESANT, ANNIE, 1847-1933

Secularist. Fabian, labour organizer, theosophist, and supporter of Indian independence, Annie Wood Besant was the daughter of a London businessman who died when she was five, and a mother who ran a boarding home for boys. She separated from her husband, a cleric, in 1873, wrote the *Gospel of Atheism* (1877), championed neo-Malthusianism, and was deprived by the courts of the custody of her children on political grounds. She joined Charles Bradlaugh in editing the *National Reformer*, and from 1883-88 published the monthly *Our Corner*, moving gradually towards socialism. In 1885 she joined the Fabians, aided in forming the Fabian Parliamentary League in 1887, and ceased to co-edit the *National Reformer* in October of that year. She participated in the November 1887 demonstration ('Bloody Sunday') at Trafalgar Square, aided in organizing the strike of female matchworkers in 1888, and served on the London School Board. In 1889 she became a theosophist, and gradually withdrew from British political activity. In the 1890s she settled in India, where she became president of the Theosophical Society from 1907 to 1933, and devoted herself after 1914 to the cause of Indian independence. She is still highly regarded in India. On her visits to London she gave speeches in support of theosophy, labour causes, and women's suffrage. See also footnotes [43] and [44].

BOLAS, THOMAS, 1848-1932

The son of a Wesleyan minister, Bolas was born in Glastonbury, Somerset and moved to London in the late 1860s, where he lived in Chiswick. He was a consulting and analytical chemist, a member of the Royal Photographic Society, the author of several books on photography, metalwork and glass-blowing, and the inventor of the 'detective camera', a box camera designed for police work.

Bolas was also interested in railway reform and printed and edited the *Railway Reformer* in 1883-84, before editing eighteen monthly issues of the Fabian newspaper *The Practical Socialist* 1886-87, and thirteen issues of *The Socialist*, 1888-89. He was one of a group which called a Fabian conference of socialists in June 1886 to sponsor parliamentary activity. He was also a member of the Hammersmith Branch SL; branch minutes list his address as 8 Grove Terrace, Chiswick, and indicate that he was an active member and was deputed to attend to printing tasks. Bolas apparently objected to the fact that in May 1888 *Commonweal* failed to publish a letter in which he complained of authoritarianism in the executive, and on 16

May he distributed a circular giving his views, in which he criticised 'parliamentarianism,' defined idiosyncratically as the limiting of free discussion among the branches (AIIS 01344, 172). *Commonweal* for 21 January 1888 records Bolas's lecture to the Clerkenwell Branch on 'A Real People's Parliament', and his circular on the same topic was published by the League in 1888. He published many leaflets on railway reform, among them: *The Chiswick Level Crossing Fatality*, Chiswick 1901, and *Confiscation of All Railway Property, as a leading step in solving the railway problem* (revised reprint from *Liberty*, The Leaflet Press, 1895). *The Labour Annual* of 1895 states that in 1893 Bolas

> resumed crusade against railway mismanagement... this time with definitely socialistic aims... now... advocates national-ization by confiscation of all railway property, so largely used as a means of extortion and plunder; to this end urges workers to secure control of legislature. (p. 163)

He was secretary of the Railway Users Association, and by 1895 lived at 60 Grove Park Terrace, Chiswick. He died in Kingston, Surrey in 1932.

BRADLAUGH, CHARLES, 1833–1891

Secularist, champion of free thought, editor of the *National Reformer*, and influential radical politician. Bradlaugh was prosecuted for sedition (1868–69), and for his defence of the publication of a birth control pamphlet (1876). He was elected to parliament in 1880, but refused to take a religious oath, and was excluded until 1886; even then his entry was opposed by Randolph Churchill. He became steadily more conservative in the 1880s and '90s, and as the *Diary* shows, used his considerable influence in working-men's clubs to oppose any socialist tendencies.

BROCHER, GUSTAVE, 1850–1931

A Communard and freethinker, Gustave Brocher was born in Delle, France and raised as a Fourierist. He had briefly become a priest, and after leaving the priesthood and experiencing the fall of the Paris Commune he taught in Russia before moving to London in 1875. There he was associated with Peter Lavrov's *Forward!*, Johann Most's *Freiheit*, and the brief-lived *Le Travail*, 1880–81 (libcom.org). According to George Woodcock (*Anarchism*, Cleveland, 1962, p. 252), Brocher chaired a committee to organize a London Anarchist Congress of 1881, and he later contributed articles to Henry Seymour's *The Anarchist*

(Quail, p. 258). Hammersmith Socialist Society minutes indicate that he lectured to the Branch twice in 1885 on continental topics, 'The Phalangstere' and 'The Icarian Communities', and the August 1885 *Commonweal* reports his singing of 'La Carmagnole' at the first annual League Conference.

Between 1885 and 1897 Brocher published three French translations and readers in London, and although in 1891 he moved to Lausanne, Switzerland, he apparently returned; an 1893 issue of *Freedom* lists him as a speaker, and he may have been at Mary Mowbray's funeral in 1893 (Quail, p. 127) as a representative of a 'French Anarchist Section' of the SL. From 1911 to 1918 Brocher taught at the academy of Fiume in Italy, and between 1915–18 he published several books in France on Russian topics. He edited selections of a *Dictionaire des Athées*, his pamphlet *Absurdités et atrocités de la Bible* (Editions de L'Idée Libre) appeared in 1926, and from 1918 until his death he served as editor of *La Libre Pensée*. A story by Gustave Brocher also appeared in Joseph Ishill's *Free Vistas* (Berkeley Heights, New Jersey 1937, vol. 2, pp. 119-30); entitled 'A Brave Parisian Lad', it records an old man's memory of the brutal shooting of a young anarchist who had given water to two National Guardsmen during the days of the Paris Commune. Brocher married Victorine Rouchy (1838–1921) in 1887, and the couple adopted five orphans of the Commune (libcom.org).

CARRUTHERS, JOHN, 1836-1914

A construction engineer, early Socialist theorist, and Morris's close associate in the SL Hammersmith Branch, Carruthers had worked on government construction projects in Egypt, India, New Zealand, Venezuela, and Argentina. He was the author of one of the first British Communist texts, *Communal and Commercial Economy* (1883), *The Political Economy of Socialism* (1885), *Socialism and Radicalism* (1894), and a posthumous *Economic Studies* (1915); he also accompanied Morris on his last visit to Norway in the summer of 1896, and left reminiscences of the voyage. His *Communal and Commercial Economy*, which argues against the wasteful competition of capitalism, and for a completely labour-based assessment of value, deserved a wider audience than it received. At times, Carruthers's views resemble Morris's:

> The system must be abolished at once... we must not wait until factories are burning and capitalists are being shot... A very few years will show the men how mistaken is their trust in strikes,

John Carruthers (from: John Carruthers, *Economic Studies*,
London: Chiswick Press, 1915)

and they will then, without delay or warning, turn to violence,
the only weapon left to them, in order to wring from the State
the rights to which they are justly entitled. No one can foretell
when this may happen; it may be in fifty years, it may be next
year, and even to-day an eloquent man could raise a tumult in
England that no human force could quell. In any case, whether
or not there is a danger or rather hope, that the working classes
are on the eve of asserting their rights, it is the duty of every
honest statesman to remove... a wrong... the only hindrance to
an almost boundless increase in human happiness. (pp. 355-56)

Carruthers' often-repeated argument that capitalism treats workers as
machinery is noted with approval in the *Diary* (see fn. [114]). Morris
presumably liked Carruthers not only for his intelligence, but for a

kindred directness, resistance to reformism, and hope for deep social transformation. For example, in an 1894 pamphlet, *Socialism and Radicalism*, Carruthers argues against agitation for Radical and labourite demands:

> ... it is inevitable that every Socialist who begins to agitate for Radicalism shall become a Radical. Therefore, I hold, it is better for us who are Socialists to continue to preach our doctrines, but not to take part in political quarrels unless we can do so independently of existing parties who, however much they may differ in other matters, are agreed in deadly hatred of Socialism. (p. 8)

Like Morris, Carruthers hoped that greater working-class boldness and consequent collapse of class structure would satisfy lesser goals:

> It is not, however, a question of half a loaf or no bread, for it is just as easy to get the whole of the loaf as the half of it, if only we could make up our minds that we really wanted the whole. (pp. 4-5)

See also footnote [114].

CHAMPION, HENRY HYDE, 1859–1928

A strange mixture of manipulator, agitator, and reformist journalist and politician, Champion was born to an upper-class family in Poona, India and educated at Marlborough College and the Royal Military College at Woolwich. At the age of twenty-three he resigned a commission in the artillery, reportedly due to his disapproval of the Egyptian War of 1882 (May Morris, *AWS*, 2:91), bought a press from which he issued socialist writings, and became the first secretary of the SDF. His reputation was tarnished when along with Maltman Barry he was accused of using Conservative Party funds to support SDF candidates in the 'Tory Gold' scandal of 1885. Champion was active in organising demonstrations of the unemployed in 1886 and 1887, and in May 1887 started *Common Sense* (and in 1888, the *Labour Elector*), which advocated immediate reforms, including the eight-hour day, adult suffrage, and free secondary education. Morris does not seem to have made many comments about him; in a 25 December 1884 letter to James L. Joynes, he remarked:

> Champion indeed thinks he can turn [Hyndman] his way, but to speak plainly I think it is just the other way. (Kelvin 2:356, BL Add. MS. 45,345)

H. H. Champion (from Joe Burgess, *John Burns:*
The Rise and Progress of a Right Honourable, Glasgow, 1911)

By late 1887 Champion was criticising Hyndman for some of the tactics which had alienated Morris — unrealistic appeal to physical force and rule by faction. In late 1887 Champion joined the Labour Electoral Association; in 1888 he was expelled from the SDF; and in 1889 he co-operated with Tom Mann and others in organising the strike of London dockers. He combined reformist Marxism with curious impulses of militarism (in an 1888 *Pall Mall Gazette* interview he spoke of the desire to shoot looters himself, scorn for most working-class leaders with whom he associated, and determination to maintain Conservative Party allies). After an abortive attempt at strike negotiation in Melbourne,

Australia in 1890–91, a failed parliamentary candidacy in Aberdeen in 1892, and his subsequent repudiation by the ILP, he left again for Australia in 1894. There he continued to work as a journalist, issued a journal, *The Champion*, wrote *The Root of the Matter* (1895), ran unsuccessfully for the Victorian Legislative Assembly, and served on the executive of the Socialist Party. In 1898 he married Elsie Goldstein, and in association with her Book Lovers' Library published a literary magazine, the *Book Lover*. Like Hyndman, Champion mixed authoritarianism and repellent elements of class-snobbery with devotion to his cause. A sympathetic modern treatment is provided by John Barnes, 'Gentleman Crusader: Henry Hyde Champion in the Early Socialist Movement', *History Workshop Journal* 60.1(2005): 116-38; Barnes suggests that the protagonist of Margaret Harkness's 1905 *George Eastmont: Wanderer* is a fictionalized representation of Champion at the time of the 1889 London dockers' strike.

CHARLES, HENRY F., 1860–1926

Henry Francis Otto Charles was born in Germany but by the mid-1880s had emigrated to London, where he lived in Camden/Kentish Town and worked briefly as a commercial traveller. An anti-parliamentarian member of the North London SL, he served as League financial secretary from December 1884 to November 1885 and on the League Council 1885–87. The 8 May 1886 *Commonweal* 'List of League Lecturers and Their Subjects' (p. 48) lists Charles as a speaker on 'State Socialism, Socialism and Anarchism', 'Society versus State Bourgeoisism', and 'Development of the German Labour Movement'. In 1886 he was responsible for bringing the Council information on police spy Karl Theodor Reuss, and after travelling to and eventually moving to the United States he contributed a series of nearly sixty 'Letters from America' to *Commonweal* from August 1887 to April 1890, listing his addresses successively as New York, Chicago, Newark, New Jersey and Boston. E.P. Thompson notes that Charles 'was an exceptionally gifted correspondent and his forthright accounts rose at times to high nobility of feeling'. (*WM*, 1955, p. 592)

Several of Charles's other letters and articles survive. In the 18 October 1884 *Justice*, (issue 40, p. 6), for example, he attacks the American ambassador, James Russell Lowell, for claiming that American democracy has been on the whole a success. And in an October 1886 letter to the *Anarchist Communist and Revolutionary* (issue 20, p. 3), he defends himself from the charge that he had acted hastily to condemn Karl Theodor Reuss, for it had been necessary 'to act in a prompt and energetic fashion to save men who were anxiously "wanted" by the Continental Police.' In this instance, of course, Charles had acted correctly. His article in the 7 February 1887 *Commonweal*, 'Peace and War' (p. 44), argues that socialists must prepare for violence: 'the better prepared for action, the more peaceable will be the revolution.'

In November 1885 Charles wrote to the SL Council to resign his post as the League's financial secretary, expressing frustration at its centralizing tendencies. Moreover he felt that the SL had been extravagant at Morris's expense: 'I believe the only way of getting out of the present stew is by devoting energy and enthusiasm to the branch and in order to do so I cannot afford to have constantly before my eyes the ghastly spectre of being engaged in pauperizing the man who is the firmest and warmest supporter of the people's cause.' (SLA 1048/1, 8 Camden St., NW) On 26 May 1886 he wrote to Halliday Sparling from Aachen, Germany to thank him for forwarding the issue of *Commonweal* which had reported the news of Reuss's expulsion, and recorded wryly that in his uncongenial occupation as a commercial traveller he has been 'telling as many lies in one minute as an ordinary person is forced to tell in a lifetime.' (SLA 1051/4). In his final letter of resignation from his position from the League Council dated 21 March, 1887, shortly before his departure for the United States, Charles states that his inability to continue results from 'the unfortunate turn my private circumstances have taken of late,' for he is not only 'without visible means of subsistence but without actual means of subsistence' (SLA 1048/1, 34 Caversham St., NY).

Three days after this letter Charles married Annette ('Nettie') Mier (1863–1946), the daughter of a Birmingham merchant, and the couple left for the United States, where their first son, Francis, was born in Chicago in 1888. There Charles assisted with the Chicago anarchist paper, *The Alarm*, formerly edited by Alfred Parsons, executed following the Haymarket Affair. The paper had closed after Parsons' arrest, but was reopened November 1887. Articles by Charles appeared on the topics of 'An Active Resistance: The Question of Combatting Unjust Conditions... ' (21 and 28 July 1888); 'A Question of Force: A Further Discussion of the Methods of Resistance to Exploitation' (8 September 1888); and 'A Text and a Source' (22 September 1888). In all of these Charles advocated armed resistance, a bold stance in view of the recent arrests. Morris's 'The Tables Turned' was reprinted between 29 September 1888 and 17 November 1888, and an article from H. Halliday Sparling on 'Our English Cousins' was featured on 11 August 1888 (p. 1). Between May 1888 and its closure in February 1889 *The Alarm* was published in New York, and for his June 1888 *Commonweal* 'Letter from America' Charles gave his address as Newark, New Jersey.

During 1888 Charles seems also to have assisted with the Chicago *Arbeiter Zeitung*, for a 14 May 1888 article in the *Lincoln* [Illinois] *Daily News* describing a meeting held to raise funds for anarchist Johann Most (then appealing a one-year prison sentence) notes that Charles had been appointed to this newspaper on Most's recommendation. According to the article, Charles spoke in German, praising Most for his advocacy of the rights of the people, and asserting that he was 'the best-hated man of two continents, the one leading champion of the white slaves of America' (p. 3).

In 1892 Charles and his family were recorded in the New York census as living in Brooklyn, with his occupation listed as 'reporter.' An article in the New York *Sun* 6 August 1896, 'Bare Feet in the Grass', identifies Henry Charles as the leader of the Kneipp-Verein, No. 1, formed to promote the medical therapies of Bavarian Abbe Sebastian Kneipp, and includes a letter in which Charles petitions city officials to permit group members to walk in Central Park, once again giving his address as Newark, New Jersey. The 1900 US census recorded Charles as living in Brooklyn with Nettie and three children born in the US (Francis, as mentioned; Alice, born in Boston, 1890; and Percy, born in NY, 1894), with an occupation of 'publisher'. The 1905 New York census described him as a 'book publisher', now in Queens, and the US 1910 census as a 'newspaper publisher', again in Brooklyn, but by 1920 he was again a 'salesman', residing in Brooklyn with his wife, three children, and a daughter-in-law. The family apparently moved to Washington, D. C., where Henry Charles died at the age of sixty-six on 3 July 1926; his death certificate lists a residence of Arkansas Avenue, N.W. Annette Charles survived him, dying in Manhattan in 1946. See also footnotes [94] and [157]. [source: Stephen Williams]

COLE, ALAN SUMMERLY, 1846–1934

Alan Cole worked as private secretary to his father (Henry Cole, Director of the Department of Science and Art, and founder of the South Kensington Museum) and as lecturer on art and promoter of Irish lacemaking, design, and drawing. During the period of the *Diary* he was the SKM's specialist for embroideries, tapestries, and textiles, and compiled several catalogues of these works acquired by the Museum during his advisorship, including *A Descriptive Catalogue of Tapestry and Embroidery in the South Kensington Museum* (1888) and *A Renascence of the Irish Art of Lace-making.* (1888).

COLINS, JEAN HIPPOLYTE, 1783–1859

A Belgian advocate of 'rational' socialism and author of several works, among them *Qu'est-ce que la science sociale* (1854–55) and a multi-volume *La science sociale* (1857–96), Colins advocated universal state-controlled guaranteed education, with an equal allowance, or dot, to be given to all upon maturity, state ownership of land and most resources, with rental to private individuals with thirty-year leases, and strict rules limiting the right of inheritance. As a middle group between the Proudhonian individualists and the communists, Colins's followers were called 'collectivists'. Colins's stress on education and collective ownership had some effect on subsequent socialist thought, and his principles were revived in the 1880s under the leadership of Frederick Borde, editor of the journal *Philosophie de L'avenir.*

COWEN, JOSEPH, 1829-1900

The son of an industrialist MP, Cowen was a radical Newcastle reformer, editor, and member of parliament. In the 1850s and '60s he supported European revolutionary movements, and was probably involved in an

Joseph Cowen 1881 (Courtesy of the National Portrait Gallery)

attempt to assassinate Napoleon III. He founded the Northern Reform Union, which advocated manhood suffrage and vote by ballot, and was proprietor of the reformist *Newcastle Daily Chronicle*, standard reading of the Northumberland working classes; he also established a co-operative store with an educational fund and library, and supported the nine-hour-day miners' strike of 1871. In 1873 he was elected to parliament as a Liberal; he was distrusted by Gladstone and other parliamentary Liberals, and defected in 1881 to oppose Irish Coercion. At one time he served as chairman for Hyndman's nascent Democratic Federation, though he soon resigned, but he kept up personal contacts with Hyndman and other leftists. Cowen became an increasingly bitter opponent of the Liberals, and in 1886 when he was returned to parliament at the top of the poll on the basis of Tory and Irish votes, he decided to retire. He continued to manage the *Newcastle Daily Chronicle*, and became increasingly imperialist in his last years. See also footnote [185].

CUNNINGHAME-GRAHAM, ROBERT BONTINE, 1852–1936

In some ways Cunninghame-Graham's career parallels Morris's. He too came from a wealthy background, and was a writer, traveller, and leftist politician, though not in the same sequence as Morris. Educated at Harrow and Brussels, he travelled in South and Central America and entered Parliament in 1886 as a Liberal MP, serving until 1892. As a kind of forerunner of a parliamentary socialist, he was completely unique in that body at the time; in particular, he advocated free secular education, the eight-hour working day, and the nationalisation of industry. He and Morris seem to have respected each other with reservations. In February 1887, Morris wrote to Jenny with irritation:

> By the way I have just got a letter from that MP again: it is headed private and most confidential, but as it is so badly written that it takes 3 strong men to read it I *must* get some one to help me. (18 February, Kelvin 2:619, BL 45,339)

(The handwriting of a Cunninghame-Graham letter to Morris in BL 45,345 confirms the source of Morris's frustration.) Later, on 18 March 1887 he wrote to Glasier:

> Cunninghame-Graham is a very queer creature, and 1 can't easily make him out; he seems ambitious; and has some decent information. (Kelvin 2:629)

R. B. Cunninghame-Graham 1890
(Courtesy of the Victoria and Albert Museum)

Likewise Cunninghame-Graham's remarks on Morris's speaking manner reflect reservations:

> ... when he spoke in public, his relatively weak voice and halting speech astonished me, and you felt, perhaps, his place would have been, then as now, beside the harpers in the hall... His speech was not convincing, but most enthusiastic in its quality. (Intro. to Arthur Compton-Rickett, *William Morris: A Study in Personality*, London 1913, p. x)

On Bloody Sunday in November 1887, Cunninghame-Graham was arrested and jailed for six weeks. After this he was ostracised by his parliamentary associates, and turned to an active career as explorer and writer, publishing more than fourteen books. In later life he espoused Scottish nationalism, and became president of the National Party of Scotland and the Scottish National Party. See also footnote [47].

DAVE, VICTOR, 1845–1922

An articulate and multilingual Belgian journalist, Dave was born in Jambes, Belgium and attended university at the Faculty of Letters in Liège and the Free University in Brussels. He joined the Brussels Federation of the International Working Men's Association and worked closely with the German Socialist movement from 1865–73, but was converted to Bakunist-Proudhonist anarchism, and became a close associate of Johann Most. After his expulsion from France in 1880 and imprisonment in Germany for his activities from 1881–84, Dave moved to London, where his more collectivist anarchism was opposed by the anarcho-communist Josef Peukert. Dave and Peukert led rival factions, which fought bitterly over Peukert's trust of Theodor Reuss. Though Reuss was later unmasked as a police spy, both Dave and Peukert were discredited by the dispute. A member of the North London SL, Dave often offered French lessons in *Commonweal* and from time to time contributed to *Commonweal*'s section of 'International News.' He collaborated in 1886 with Bax and Morris on a pamphlet about the Paris

Victor Dave (Courtesy of Ateneu Llibertari Estel Negre, Palma, Majorca)

Commune and published an obituary of French dramatist and Communard Felix Pyat in the August 1889 *Commonweal*.

Later Dave returned to France and in 1897 assumed editorship of the anarchist paper *L'Humanité nouvelle*; in 1900 the *Labour Annual* listed his address as 19, rue de Boulainvilliers, Paris. In the same year he published in Paris a pamphlet on Bakunin and Marx; in 1903 with an associate he published two translations from Lassalle and a brief life of French anarcho-syndicalist Fernand Pelloutier; and in 1903–1904 he co-edited the *Revue générale de bibliographie française*. In *Living My Life* (New York 1931), Emma Goldman records her favourable impression of Dave during a visit to Paris around 1900:

> He was kindly and jovial. Though sixty [in 1900 he would have been fifty-five], he was as alert in mind and spirit as in his student days. Eking out a meagre existence as contributor to anarchist and other publications, he yet retained the buoyancy and humour of youth. I spent much time with him and his lifelong companion, Marie, an invalid for many years, but still interested in public affairs... The most fascinating thing about Victor Dave was his innate feeling for life and ready enjoyment of fun. He was the freest and gayest among the many comrades I met in Paris, a companion after my own heart. (vol. 1, pp. 266-67)

After 1909 he worked as a proofreader, and during WWI, unlike most anarchists he joined Kropotkin in supporting the Allied cause. He died in Paris in 1922. See also footnotes [56]–[58].

DONALD, ALEXANDER KARLEY, MA, 1859–1917

Born in Kincardine, Scotland, Donald obtained an arts degree from the University of Edinburgh. After moving to London he joined the Socialist League in 1885 and became a leader of its parliamentary faction. In 1889 he married Helen Gostling, the daughter of former Bloomsbury SL members David and Sarah Gostling, also parliamentarians. Donald wrote for *Commonweal* and spoke frequently; the *Diary* indicates that Morris considered him a good speaker. He also thought him 'a regular intriguer and no good in any association either...' (letter to Henry Charles, 16 June, 1887, Kelvin 2:669; Houghton Library). In 1888 Donald left the League in the secession of parliamentarians to join the Labour Emancipation League, and in 1889 he attended the Paris Congress of the Socialist International on behalf of the Hoxton Labour

League; this became the Labour Union, in which Donald was a prominent member. In an 1891 letter to Bruce Glasier in which he commented on Donald's post-secession activities, Morris noted:

> A great deal of our trouble comes from Messrs Donald and Mahon who have been rather clever at pulling us to pieces, but could do nothing towards building up even their own humbugging self-seeking party. (6 April, Kelvin 3:51)

and in another 1890 letter he used language as sharp as any of which he was capable to comment on the Bloomsbury Branch expulsion:

> They deserved it, for it was that pig of a Donald who began it all. (5 December 1890, Kelvin 3:239)

In 1890, along with John L. Mahon and Tom Binning, Donald led a failed postal strike for the Labour Union of Hoxton; later, he became a founding member of the ILP, but was expelled along with Aveling and Mahon. (Paul Thompson, *Socialists, Liberals, and Labour*, London 1967, p. 161) In 1892 he ran as a Labour Union candidate in the 1892 general election in the Shoreditch, Hoxton constituency, where he polled only seventeen votes. No one seems to have recorded any praiseful recollections which counterbalance Morris's opinion. Yvonne Kapp speaks of him as retired from political activity by 1898 (*Eleanor Marx*, vol. 2, p. 717), and in 1895 and 1902 he edited texts for the Early English Text Society.

Donald became a barrister in 1897, and in 1902 was appointed Professor of Law at the Government Law School in Bombay, where his father-in-law headed an architectural and engineering firm. In 1905 Donald became Second Judge in the Bombay Court of Second Cause, and after 1908 acting Chief Judge in that court. He also joined David and Sarah Gostling in the Bombay Fabian Society. Donald returned to England in 1917 and died in West Dulwich shortly afterwards. (I am indebted to Stephen Williams for much of this information.)

FAULKNER, CHARLES JOSEPH, 1834–92

A gifted mathematician and one of Morris's closest lifelong friends, Faulkner came from Birmingham and met Morris at Oxford, where Faulkner earned two firsts in mathematics and a first in natural science. He was a member of the Oxford group who issued the *Oxford and Cambridge Magazine* in 1856, joined Rossetti, Morris and others in the 'jovial campaign' to paint the Oxford Union Murals in 1857, served as

Charles J. Faulkner
aet 24

Charles Faulkner (Courtesy of the National Portrait Gallery)

best man at Morris's wedding, and became a founding member of Morris, Marshall, Faulkner and Co. (later Morris and Co.). He was elected a Fellow of University College in 1856, and after an absence in London to keep books for the Firm, he returned to the College, where he held positions as lecturer in mathematics 1864–71 and Senior Fellow 1877–92, along with administrative posts as bursar, dean, registrar, and librarian.

Faulkner accompanied Morris to Iceland in 1871, joined him in a Workman's Neutrality Demonstration in 1878, founded the Oxford branch of the Socialist League, and in 1885 contributed £100 to the inauguration of *Commonweal*. Faulkner's efforts on behalf of socialism drew some local opprobrium; in 1885 the *Oxford Magazine* described his views as 'alehouse anarchism,' and hostile undergraduates christened a donkey 'Comrade Faulkner' after their College librarian and Dean of Degrees. Even the *Daily Telegraph* objected when Faulkner joined Morris in supporting the defenders of Khartoum against General Gordon: 'He denounces public men all around[, asserting that] Colonel

Burnaby [a calvary officer killed in the attempt to retake Kartoum] — for even death does not disarm his criticism — was a scoundrel.'

In the summer of 1887 he published an article in *Commonweal*, 'Inhuman Arithmetic', attacking political economy for reducing men to ciphers. Like Morris's other prosperous socialist friend Philip Webb, Faulkner was anti-parliamentarian and tended towards vague declarations of anti-capitalism. In 'Law and War', which appeared in the *Commonweal* issue for 7 January 1888 and the two succeeding weeks, he asserted (as did Morris) that 'we shall not be flurried by the thought of the great struggle which shall put an end to it all'. A letter from Faulkner to Joseph Lane of 18 May 1887 commenting on Lane's *Anti-Statist Communist Manifesto* argues against its direct attacks on religion and expounds a kind of libertarian anarchism:

> ... what we wish to do is destroy authority, and among other authorities that will disappear will be those who pretend to know more than others about 'the next world' and about 'god'... we may safely leave all men to speculate freely... the socialist should be free to think and to speculate on any subject whatever.... what he is forbidden to do, which is the very aim of socialism to prevent, is the interfering with other people... (BL Add. MS. 46,345)

Faulkner's closeness to Morris was described by their mutual friend Philip Webb in a letter to J. W. Mackail, 4 June 1898:

> ... I can answer in a dependable way as to the friendship to the last between the two men: assuredly it was that of the greatest confidence and affection. The unbreakable courage and clear honesty of Faulkner held Morris as closely as friendship, pure and simple, could bind two men together — regardless of difference in quality of mind. They each did for the other what they could not have done for anyone else; and I had the good luck to be alive to this perfect love. C.J.F. had the capacity of seeing the value of that towards which he had no natural attraction; and this, to me, seems to be one of the rarest fine qualities. (WMorris Gal, J170)

To his friend and biographer W. R. Lethaby, Philip Webb noted that Faulkner had been 'the man of the clearest honesty' he had known. 'He was most invincibly kind, loyal and persistent and Morris's truest follower.' (Lethaby, *Philip Webb and His Work*, 1935, 246). Faulkner's sister Kate was a designer for Morris and Co., and the Faulkners were frequent guests of the Morrises. Faulkner was paralysed in October

1888, although he did not die until 1892; his loss was a severe blow to Morris in an already discouraging period of his life. [See also William Whyte, 'Charles J. Faulkner,' *ODNB*, and Tony Pinkney, *William Morris in Oxford: The Campaigning Years*, 1874–1895, Illuminati, 2007].

FIELDING, JOHN, 1848–1932?

Born in Bradford, Fielding moved to London where he worked as a shorthand transcriber. He was an active SDF propagandist; H. Lee remembered him as an able speaker (*Social Democracy in Britain*, 1935, p. 100) and the 4 July 1885 *Justice* 'Lecture Diary' lists him as one of twelve available speakers, with lectures on 'The Malthusian Nightmare', 'Internationalism', 'Christianity and Socialism', and several other topics. In the first election contested by the SDF, in November 1885, Fielding was a defeated candidate for Kennington against O'Connor Power, polling only thirty-two votes. Fearful of losing his London employment, Fielding devoted much of his energy to provincial recruitment. See also footnote [181].

FOOTE, GEORGE WILLIAM, 1850–1915

A radical reformer, Foote had been a religious youth, converted to freethinking through the writings of Ruskin, Darwin, Carlyle, and Mill. On moving from Plymouth to London in 1868 he founded the Young Men's Secular Association, joined the National Secular Society, and contributed to the *National Reformer*. After briefly partnering with G.J. Holyoake in 1876 to found the short-lived *The Secularist*, in 1877 he began the editorship of the *Freethinker*. In 1883 he was imprisoned for one year at hard labor for alleged 'blasphemy', and on his release issued a memoir, *Prisoner for Blasphemy* (1886). A radical and land-nationaliser, Foote remained opposed to socialism. When Bradlaugh resigned as president of the National Secular Society in 1890, Foote was his successor. See also footnotes [43] and [45].

GLASIER, J. BRUCE, 1859–1920

After the death of his father at age thirteen, Glasier grew up in near-poverty in Glasgow, where as an adolescent he served an apprenticeship as an architectural draughtsman. As an agitator he was unable to work at his trade and became a decorative iron designer. He began to write verses, sending copies to Morris and other contemporary poets. In 1881 Glasier joined the Irish Land League and in 1884 he helped found the

John Bruce Glasier (from *Labour Annual*, ed. Joseph Edwards, 1895)

Glasgow branch of the SDF, following Morris into the SL in 1885, and serving as SL Glasgow branch secretary. In the latter capacity he arranged for Morris's speaking visits in Glasgow, and his 1921 *William Morris and the Early Days of the Socialist Movement* is a pleasant if rather lightweight evocation of these visits. Its effort to present Morris as uninterested in Marxism have drawn upon it highly charged and heavily documented attacks by E.P. Thompson and Paul Meier, but Glasier's book seems to me insufficiently pointed to merit such artillery. Its Morris is a rather vaguely hearty well-wisher to Glasier, not a serious theoretician of any kind. More than anything else, Glasier's book testifies convincingly to Morris's ability to enjoy the company of almost all his coworkers, and to hearten, even inspire, the insecure and lonely young author.

Glasier censored the letters from Morris which he printed; the originals in the William Morris Gallery indicate that Morris was often distressed at the Glasgow branch's unwillingness to sell *Commonweal*, pay back debts, or keep current with dues. Glasier also omits the occasion of much of Morris's interest, his concern that the Glasgow branch should maintain its anti-parliamentary stance. Later Glasier became a supporter of the ILP and propagandist for the opposite point of view. Glasier wrote several pamphlets and a book of socialist songs. In 1893 he married a Cambridge graduate and Fabian lecturer, Katharine Conway, with whom he visited Morris and the Hammersmith Socialist Society; he co-authored *The Religion of Socialism* (1894), and spent a lifetime of preaching an ethical version of socialism and campaigning for the ILP. Glasier served on the ILP Council, edited the *Labour Leader*, opposed labour support of World War I, and fought against union with the SDF. His memoirs of Morris, written before his death, were edited by Katharine Conway Glasier.

GLASSE, JOHN, MA, 1848–1918

Born in Auchtermuchty and educated at St. Andrews University and New College, Edinburgh, Glasse served as minister of Old Greyfriars Church, Edinburgh, from 1877 to 1909. He became a prominent advocate of Christian Socialism, an active Freemason, president of the Edinburgh Burns Club, and an early member of the SDF, Socialist League, and ILP. His 'Harvest Hymn' appeared in Edward Carpenter's *Chants of Labour* (1888), and he was the author of several pamphlets on Christian Socialism and *John Knox: A Critique and an Appreciation* (1905), which argued that Knox's message required updating to address poverty in an industrial age. A discussion of his views appears in Michael A. McCabe, 'The Tears of the Poor: John Glasse, Christian Socialist (1848-1918)', *Records of the Scottish Church History Society* 28 (1998): 149-72. See also footnote [134].

HENDERSON, JAMES FREDERICK (FRED), 1868–1957

Born the son of a Norwich clothier, and educated at the Belfast Mercantile Academy and Owen's College, Manchester, Henderson returned to Norwich and founded a branch of the Socialist League in 1886. At the time of his arrest and imprisonment in Norwich Castle for speaking to the unemployed, he was nineteen years old; at sixteen, he had published the first of three volumes of poems, and in 1887 he issued *Echoes of the Coming Day: Socialist Songs and Rhymes*. When in the late 1880s he went to London and worked as a reporter for the *Star*, he stayed for a time at Morris's Kelmscott House. Joining Mahon in an attempt to form an independent labour party, he founded the Clapham Labour League with its journal the *Labour Leader*, and in 1892 he was elected in Clapham as one of six successful socialist candidates for the London

Fred Henderson (Courtesy of the Norfolk Public Library)

County Council. Later in the '90s he returned to Norwich, where he worked as a journalist, and in 1902 was elected the first socialist member of the City Council. When women became eligible for civic office, he and his wife became the first married couple in England to serve together on the same local governing body. Henderson worked as an alderman from 1923, and later during the Second World War he served as chairman of the Norwich Food Control Committee, and briefly in 1939–40 as Lord Mayor of the city where as a youth he had been imprisoned. Described as an eloquent and effective speaker, Henderson wrote several books on socialism, including the widely circulated *The Case for Socialism* (1911), *The New Faith: A Study of Party Politics and the War* (1915), and *Money Power and Human Life* (1932). A three-page bibliography of his writings and their foreign translations appeared in the *Norwich Public Libraries Readers' Guide*, vol. XII, no.9, accompanied by a picture of Henderson as mayor in 1939. See also footnote [3].

HOGG, WILLIAM BRUCE GORDON, 1849–1915

Born in Jamaica, Gordon Hogg studied at St. Andrews University and received his M.D. from the University of Edinburgh in 1873. After moving to London he practiced medicine in Ealing and Chiswick, where he was elected to the Chiswick Improvement Committee and Chiswick Local Health Board. The *West London Observer* for 1887 indicates that Dr Gordon Hogg was a trustee of the expanding Chiswick Liberal Club, which moved to larger premises in November 1887. During the year Tom Mann, Hyndman, Annie Besant, and Morris spoke to the club, and Dr Hogg frequently chaired meetings. In 1885 he had tried unsuccessfully for parliament as a Liberal in the Ealing constituency; on 30 April the *WLO* records a speech regretting the 'defeat of their worthy candidate, Dr Hogg'. The 12 March *WLO* gives a precis of Dr Hogg's views at a club debate:

> The true causes, he said, of the present depression had not been fully stated by the recent Royal Commission; it was not overproduction, but lack of purchasing power on the part of the people. But curious to say that while there was this poverty among the people, the wealth of the world was increasing, showing that some people were obtaining more than their share. (p. 5)

His proposed non-socialist remedies included restriction of continental loans and return of labourers to the countryside. However, he apparently modified these views, for in autumn 1887 he applied to become a member of the Socialist League, listing his address as Bedford Park.

HOWARD, GEORGE 1843–1911 and ROSALIND STANLEY HOWARD, 1845–1920

George Howard was a landscape watercolourist, Liberal MP for East Cumberland 1879–80 and 1881–85, and after 1885, eighth Earl of Carlisle and Liberal Unionist member of the House of Lords; later, he also became a trustee of the National Gallery. His wife Rosalind Howard, described by the *D.N.B.* as 'an ardent public worker on the radical side', administered their vast estates while he devoted himself to painting and an interest in Italian art and culture. As close friends of the Burne-Joneses, their social life overlapped the Morrises'; the firm did decorating work for the Howards' London home in Holland Park, Naworth Castle in Cumberland, and Castle Howard in Yorkshire; and George Howard and Morris worked together for the Society for the Protection of Ancient Buildings. George's health was one reason for the Howards' frequent trips to Italy, Egypt, and other warm climates. Jane Morris became their friend, accompanying them on extended trips and visiting them at Castle Howard. As wealthy patrons of the arts and Mediterranean travellers sympathetic to health constraints, they would have been congenial companions for Jane and Jenny. In an 1881 letter during an earlier trip Morris wrote jokingly to his wife, 'Good bye, my dear, take care of yourself: and *please* pay your way duly to Mrs. Howard: I can't go owing money to Earl-Kin' (17[?] February, Kelvin 2:21). Jane Morris's letters in the Castle Howard Archives reveal some embarrassment at her husband's tendency to argue politics with Rosalind Howard, and a deep affection for and gratitude to the latter for many kindnesses to herself and Jenny (see esp. Sharp and Marsh, *Letters of JM*, nos. 8, 37, and 44). In later life Rosalind became an active campaigner for women's suffrage and temperance. See also footnotes [39] and [50].

HYNDMAN, HENRY MAYERS, 1842–1921

Founder and leader of the Social Democratic Federation, Hyndman's paradoxical combination of authoritarian arrogance and socialist conviction left its impression on early British socialism. Born to a prosperous family of colonial connections, Hyndman attended Trinity College, Cambridge, studied for the bar, and travelled in Italy, Australia, and the US. He early developed a belief that the need for a strong British empire required greater opportunities for native autonomy. After a failed attempt to run for Parliament as a Liberal, Hyndman read *Das Kapital* in French translation, and made use of some of its ideas without acknowledgment in *Textbook for Democracy: England for All* (1881), and, with acknowledgment, in *The Historical Basis for Socialism* (1883). Marx was skeptical of his disciple, describing him as 'self-satisfied and querulous'. (letter to Sorge, Marx and Engels, *Correspondence, 1846–1895*, 1934, p. 397)

In 1881 Hyndman helped found the Democratic Federation, which Morris joined in 1883 and which became the Social Democratic Federation in 1884. The SDF soon divided over Hyndman's jingoism, his desire for absolute control, and his emphasis on parliamentarianism, parades, and threats to the civil authorities. In 1885 Morris led a disaffected wing out of the organization to form the Socialist League, and stated his objection to Hyndman's tactics as follows:

> … his aim has been to make the movement seem big; to frighten
> the powers that be with a turnip bogie which perhaps he almost
> believes in himself: hence all that insane talk of immediate
> forcible revolution, when we know that the workers in England
> are not even touched by the movement; hence the founding of

branches which melt away into mere names, the neglect of organisation for fruitless agitation; and worst of all, hence discreditable intrigue and sowing of suspicion among those who are working for the party. Amidst such elements as this I cannot and will not work, and they are the only elements amongst which H. will work... (letter Joynes, Christmas Day 1884, Kelvin 2:356, BL Add. MS 45,345)

Later Hyndman moved from these stances to parliamentarianism and mild trade union agitation. He led the SDF until 1912, its offshoot, the British Socialist Party (BSP), from 1912 to 1917, and a group of pro-war dissidents from the BSP, the National Socialist Party (NSP), from 1917 to 1919. When the BSP merged into the Communist Party after World War I, the 2,000 member NSP/SDF affiliated with the Labour Party. He died in 1921. Hyndman wrote a brief memoir of Morris for *Justice* in 1896, later reprinted as a pamphlet. His memories praise Morris's character, but blur his political views.

Henry M. Hyndman (from Joe Burgess, *John Burns: The Rise and Progress of a Right Honorable*, Glasgow, 1911)

KITZ, FRANK, 1849–1923

Kitz was a radical populist, promoter of relief for the unemployed, and anarchist activist. 'Frank Kitz' was the name assumed by Francis Platt, the illegitimate child of Mary Platt and John Lewis, a watchmaker. Born in London and raised in dire poverty, he was briefly apprenticed as a dyer. During the 1870s he was an active member of several London left-radical clubs and helped shift others towards the left; in 1874 he served as secretary of the Democratic and Trades Alliance, and in 1875 of its successor, the Manhood Suffrage League; in 1877 he aided in forming an English section of the Rose St Social Democratic Club. He was a delegate to the anarchist International Revolutionary Congress in 1881, secretary of the Freiheit Defence Committee, and editor of the English version of *Freiheit*. In 1882 Kitz, Lane, and others formed the Labour Emancipation League, and in 1885 Kitz joined the SL and served on its Council several times. The unsympathetic *Daily News* reporter who attended the 1887 Paris Commune celebration described his speaking manner (18 March):

> One Frank Kitz followed him, another man of the same [low] educational rank, but fluent and measured, and with a clear sense of what he wanted to say. He was denunciatory, but always within bounds, and he could be quite angry without foaming at the mouth. He was very angry with the English Press; it pandered to the capitalist class; it was a moral policeman doing the dirty work of society... What the Commune died for was to mend such misery as the misery of our unemployed. This was the note of doctrine for the whole meeting; whenever a speaker repeated this, or something like it, he was sure of his cheer. 'Before many years have passed,' he said, in conclusion, 'we shall begin to handle the wealth which is the produce of our hands.' This earned him frantic applause.

Kitz worked for Morris at Merton Abbey and accompanied him to Paris as SL delegate to the Socialist Congress of 1889. After the parliamentarians left the League, he became its secretary 1888–91, and when Morris left he served with David Nicholl as joint editor of *Commonweal*. Things ended disastrously when in March 1891 the Hammersmith Socialist Society expelled him on a charge of absconding with SL monies and account books. *Freedom* lists him as delivering a lecture in 1895, so he probably continued some anarchist activity. He resumed propaganda as a syndicalist in 1909–1912, and published a series of 'Recollections and Reflections' in the 1912 *Freedom* (January–July). He devotes an entire issue's 'Recollections' to Morris, but his remarks are impersonal and include few specific memories. Appeals for his financial relief appeared in *Freedom* in 1920 and 1922, and *Freedom* reported, 'Now, over seventy years of age, he is no longer able to earn a living at his trade of dyer, and has only the miserable old-age pension of ten shillings weekly as a means of subsistence'. (March 1922). He died in the next year in great poverty at the age of seventy-three. See also footnote [4].

KROPOTKIN, PETER, 1842–1921

Russian revolutionist, scientist, and anarchist, Kropotkin had served as an army officer in Siberia from 1862 to 1867. During this period he studied the region's geography and plant life, but also became convinced of the need for cooperative socialism and the abolition of government. In 1871 he refused the Secretaryship of the Russian Geographical Society to devote his life to social justice. A visit to Swiss watchmakers in the Jura mountains convinced him of the efficacy of voluntary mutual aid as a form of social organisation. Imprisoned in 1876 by the Tsarist

Peter Kropotkin poss. c. 1881 (Wiki, photo by Nadar [Gaspard-Félix Tournachon])

government for promulgating his views, he escaped to Switzerland in 1876, and after expulsion by the Swiss government suffered imprisonment in France from 1883–86. He settled in England in March 1886 and began the work of publicising anarchism which was to engage him until his return to Russia in 1917; in 1885 he published *Paroles d' un revolutionnaire* and in 1887 *In Russian and French Prisons*, but he was already working at the ideas that would appear in *Fields, Factories, and Workshops* (1899). As the *Diary* indicates, Morris and Kropotkin shared platforms during this period; Kropotkin excused himself from writing for *Commonweal* on the grounds of overwork in co-editing *Le Revolte*, and *Freedom*, which he published with Charlotte Wilson from 1886. John Hulse's *Revolutionists in London* gives a good account of the parallels between Morris's and Kropotkin's thought; see also my first introduction. Long an opponent of the Prussian state, Kropotkin disappointed his fellow anarchists by supporting the Allied Powers in World War I. In 1917 at the age of seventy-five he returned to Russia, where he opposed the Bolshevik government, and worked on a history of ethics. His wife Sophie was a campaigner for women's higher education in Russia, and later a teacher. See also footnotes [61], [62] and [174].

LAFARGUE, PAUL, 1842–1911

Marxist organiser and author of several books on the relation of economics to literary, ethical, and philosophic beliefs, Lafargue studied medicine, participated in the Paris Commune, and later worked in Madrid to establish a socialist party in opposition to the Bakuninists. In 1872 he moved to London, where he married Marx's daughter Laura. In 1880 he and Jules Guesde drew up the Marxist programme of the French Workers' Party; he was later amnestied in France, and returned in 1882 to lead the party along with Guesde. He was imprisoned in 1891 for speaking at a May Day demonstration, served as the first Socialist deputy in the French Parliament from 1891–93, and in 1905, joined the newly-founded United Socialist Party.

LANE, JOSEPH, 1851–1920

An important early working-class organiser and anarchist activist, Lane was the son of a cordwainer, and came to London in 1865 or 1866. While working as a carter he joined several working-class organisations, including the English section of the Rose Street Social

Democratic Club and the Local Rights Association. In March 1881 he joined the Freiheit Defence Committee to defend the anarchist Johann Most, and helped produce several issues of an English *Freiheit*. In 1881 Lane moved to Hackney and formed a new club which became the Homerton Social Democratic Club, and which sent delegates to the anarchist International Revolutionary Congress of 1881. He joined Frank Kitz in organising open-air meetings at Mile End Waste, and with Kitz and others, he formed the Labour Emancipation League in 1882. When this merged into the SDF in 1884, Lane became a member of the SDF Council. He joined the SL in its split with the SDF, and with Morris became the co-publisher of *Commonweal*; along with Kitz, Mowbray, and Mainwaring he formed an anarchist wing of the League. The *Daily News* reporter who attended the 1887 Paris Commune celebration has left a condescending account of his speech (March 18):

> A humble sort of man, named Lane, who acted as chairman, spoke first. He took his station on the platform with a few dirty red flags to right and left of him... and he made a short introductory speech. He dropped his h's recklessly, as might have been expected; and we only mention it to show that he was in character. His theme was that the course of Communism, though crushed in 1871, was stronger than ever to-day, and that the Commune was a great advance on all previous revolutions, because it was social; while the others were only political. The next revolution, in like manner, would be a great advance on that.

Diary entries and Morris's letters to Lane indicate that Lane frequently took offence over political disputes at meetings of the Council and Conference; at one point Morris urged him not to reopen an issue on which the Council had already expressed its confidence in him (13 May 1889, Kelvin 3:61, BL 45,345). Morris paid for Lane's visit to France as League emissary to the socialist congress of 1887. Although Morris urged Lane to circulate his League policy minority report before the 1887 conference (see footnote [192]), he found it rather wordy and abstract. Lane's manifesto attacked trade unions and elections as reformist, and advocated revolutionary violence and complete abolition of the state:

> The study of history has taught us that the noblest conquests of man are written on a blood-stained book. (*An Anti-Statist Communist Manifesto*, repr. Cienfuegos Press 1978, p. 36)

When the May 1887 Conference rejected this document, Lane published it in June as *An Anti-Statist Communist Manifesto*. Even Lane had some difficulty working with the other SL anarchists who remained after the departure of the Parliamentarians from the League, and in 1889 he resigned from the SL, writing Morris an explanatory letter. Morris's response indicates his usual tact, and a sincere sense of loss:

> ... I always looked upon you as one of the serious members of the League, and that it is quite true, as far as I can see that our views as to Anarchism are very close together; and in consequence that I look upon your loss as serious in all ways...
> (21 May 1889, Kelvin 3: 68, BL 45,345)

Lane continued to publish occasional political pamphlets, and died in 1920 (for a biographical sketch, see the introduction by Nicolas Walter to *An Anti-Statist Communist Manifesto*). See also footnotes [15], [111], [139], [147], [149] and [155].

MACDONALD, JAMES, 1857–1938

A West End tailor born in Glasgow, James ('Jimmie') Macdonald came to London in 1881, where he joined the Central Marylebone Democratic Association and met Frank Kitz, Jack Williams, and other left radicals. He became one of the first members of Hyndman's Social Democratic Federation and a member of its first executive, one of the few working-class men in this group. After a brief period in the Socialist Union from 1885 to 1887, he returned to the SDF. In his July 1896 article in *Justice* for the series, 'How I Became a Socialist', Macdonald would only comment briefly on this episode:

> In 1885 I, with others, left because we disagreed with the policy pursued in regard to elections [the 'Tory Gold' scandal]. I rejoined in 1887 because I gathered from a speech of Hyndman's that that policy was practically repudiated.

During the cotton strike of 1884 Macdonald and Jack Williams organised a Blackburn SDF branch, and in 1885 he was arrested with other socialists defending free speech at Dod Street.

In 1888 Macdonald and Lewis Lyons led the agitation of a united body of East End and West End tailors which became the Amalgamated Society of Tailors. In their Macdonald entry for *The Dictionary of Labour Biography*, vol. 7, David E. Martin and James A. Schmiechen describe him as a 'close reasoner and debater with an eloquent and pleasing manner,' widely considered 'the best orator in the British tailoring trade union movement.' A foe of gradualism and promoter of socialist unity, he consistently supported policies of collective ownership as well as the inclusion of women, unskilled workers, and 'aliens' (in this context, Jews) in union membership. Macdonald's West End branch of the Amalgamated Society of Tailors was the first to admit women and 'aliens', and in 1905 it seceded from the parent union over this issue to form the London Society of Tailors and Tailoresses.

Macdonald joined the Independent Labour Party (ILP) and ran twice as its parliamentary candidate in Dundee in 1892 and 1895. He was also a member of the London Trades Council (LTC) Executive from 1890, and became its Secretary from 1896–1913, strongly influencing its socialist orientation and founding and editing its newspaper, the *London Trades and Labour Gazette*. As its representative to the Trades Union Congress in 1893 he proposed a successful resolution requiring that the TUC support only candidates who accepted the principle of collective ownership. Guided by Macdonald, the LTC campaigned for a minimum wage, municipal housing, and meals for schoolchildren. Its advocacy of unemployment relief helped lead to the Unemployed Workmen Act of 1905; the LTC also supported women unionists in their campaign for a minimum wage in sweated trades, a campaign that led to the first Trade Boards Act in 1909.

An 1896 *Justice* article describes Macdonald as 'young', and as 'a rather fair, dapper little fellow, of pleasing appearance'. In the article he describes himself as still lecturing for the SDF and other labour organisations. In 1898 he initiated talks to consider an SDF–ILP merger, but these failed when the ILP withdrew from negotiations.

In 1915 several unions joined to form the United Garment Workers' Union, which united craft and factory workers as Macdonald had advocated, and he remained secretary of the London branch until 1927. In 1914 he contributed reminiscences of Hyndman to a retrospective issue of *Justice*. After retiring Macdonald moved briefly to Australia, returning to England a few years before his death in Islington in 1938. The LTC established a memorial fund for his widow, also a member of the British Socialist Party Women's Council. See also footnote [59].

MAGUIRE, TOM, 1864–1895

A semi-employed photographer, newspaper vendor, and working-class poet from a poverty-stricken Irish Catholic background, Maguire was an active socialist before he was twenty and the first promoter of socialism in Leeds. In 1884 Maguire formed a branch of the SDF in Leeds, which in 1885 affiliated with the Socialist League and became one of its most active branches; he was a member of the first provisional Council of the SL, contributed poems to *Commonweal* later collected in *Machine-Room Chants* (1895), and continued a steady supporter of the League until Morris's departure in 1890. A skilled open-air speaker, he aided in organising an 1889 building labourers' strike in Leeds, in 1890 helped establish a Labour Electoral League, and in 1892–93 was one of the founders of the ILP. Elizabeth Miller summarizes his contribution: 'While still in his early 20s, he was a leader in instigating the tide of New Unionism—the effort to broaden the scope of organized labor to include unskilled and semi-skilled workers—that swept Leeds in a number of important strikes in 1889-1890, including dyers, gas workers, tailoresses, builders' laborers, and bricklayers.' (*Slow Print: Literary Radicalism and Victorian Print Culture*, 2013, p. 204) He continued to publish poems in

Tom Maguire (from *Tom Maguire: A Remembrance*, ed. I. Ford, Manchester Labour Press, 1895)

venues such as the *Labour Leader*, the *Leeds Labour Chronicle*, and his own short-lived *Labour Champion* (1893), often in the persona of a working-class woman speaker. Factionalism in the Leeds movement contributed to a personal depression, which helped precipitate his death from pneumonia in March 1895 at the age of thirty. More than 1000 mourners attended his funeral. In his introductory remarks on *Machine Room Chants*, J. Bruce Glasier speaks of Maguire as 'one of those men of whom we seldom meet more than one in a lifetime, who possess that indefinable charm of friendship that suffers not by passing through the furnace heat or killing cold of life's vicissitudes'. For a discussion of his poetry, see Miller, *Slow Print*, pp. 204-19.

MAHON, JOHN LINCOLN, 1865–1933

The son of Irish Catholic parents living in Edinburgh, Mahon was a former engineer and member of the Scottish Land and Labour League, who joined the SDF, served on its executive, and was the first secretary of the SL. Boycotted by employers, he began full-time campaigning for socialism in the Midlands, became a highly successful organiser of the miners, and later moved from an anti-parliamentarian to a parliamentarian position. In letters to Mahon, Morris criticised what he believed to be his tendency to stir up arguments, and throughout 1887 and 1888 his comments to Mahon are rather sharp in tone. He felt Mahon should not work as a paid political organiser, that he should recruit for the League rather than a non-League group, was irritated that he had given away rather than sold *Commonweal*, and suggested that Mahon and other SL parliamentarians should join the SDF. Mahon must have written some angry responses, because Morris was roused to reply:

> As to brags about the relative amount of work we do; let's remember the old proverb and wait till we are dead before we raise that question — and meantime do all we can. Yes, please consider my advice not because it's mine, but because it's good… I am not in the least in an ill-temper, but I am vexed that the road to *organisation* should lie through the breaking up of the League, and the snuffing out of *Commonweal*, if that must be so…

> Fraternally and good-temperedly yours, William Morris (30 July 1887, Kelvin 2:680-81)

Morris's letters of the period refer in jest to Mahon's 'cheek' and 'chin', and more seriously to Morris's belief that although Mahon stirs up ill-will, he is basically well-intended. As early as 1887 Engels referred to Mahon as involved in forming a labour party, and by 1888 Mahon had left the SL with the Labour Emancipation League to form a new Labour Union; he published a long pamphlet, *A Labour Programme*, with a preface by R. Cunninghame-Graham, and as a member of the newly formed Scottish Labour Party supported the parliamentary candidacy of Keir Hardie. In 1890 Mahon, Donald, and Binning led the Labour Union in a disastrous Postman's Union strike. By the time of the formation of the ILP he was sufficiently reformist to oppose an ILP goal of collective ownership, a position supported by the majority of delegates, and later, in another failed measure, he opposed the ILP's rejection of designated campaign funds. Ultimately he was expelled from the Leeds branch ILP. His later political career is traced in Edmund Rogers, 'From Socialism to Liberal Unionism: J. L. Mahon in Edwardian Dublin,' (*History Workshop Journal* 77 [2014], 137-59); blacklisted in Leeds, in 1898 he moved to work as a commercial chemical salesman in Ireland, where he became an opponent of Home Rule, an ally of Joseph Chamberlain, and a supporter of tariff reform, running unsuccessfully as a Liberal Unionist candidate for Parliament in 1906. He later returned to England and in the 1911 census was listed as living with his family in Lambeth, central London. Mahon became a member of May Morris's Kelmscott Fellowship in 1919, wrote Frank Kitz's obituary for *Justice* in 1923, and according to Edmund Rogers, was active as an 'anti-Bolshevik in the interwar socialist scene' (137). His son and namesake (1901–1975) later became a trade unionist and London District Secretary of the Communist Party. See also footnotes [78], [96] and [145].

MAINWARING, SAM, 1841–1907

Called by his biographer, Ken John, the first 'post-Marx' Welsh syndicalist and inventor of the label anarcho-syndicalist, the Welsh engineer and anarchist trade unionist Mainwaring was born in Heath, Wales, married a Cardiff customs officer's daughter in 1868, and worked briefly in the US before returning to London. As the engineer of a Marylebone shop and member of the Amalgamated Engineers Union, he influenced his younger co-worker, Tom Mann; later he helped found the Labour Emancipation League, joined the SDF, and left in the 1885 split to join the SL. He became an active speaker in the London parks, was arrested with Jack Williams in 1886, and fined £20; the Hammersmith Socialist Society notes record Morris's attempt to raise money for his defence. A *Commonweal* Hackney branch report of a talk Mainwaring gave in January 1887 outlines some of his views:

> He said that the revolutionary Socialist never asks for palliative measures, either from local boards, or even Parliament itself. He showed that all movements of the people against abuse or monopoly, never succeeded except through the efforts of men who rebelled against the then existing 'law and order'.

Mainwaring helped organise the League's platform at the 11 April 1887 Anti-Coercion demonstration, and later in the year he and Kitz visited South Wales coalfields on a propaganda tour. In 1891 he returned to South Wales to help raise two children deserted by his brother Tom, Ellen and Sam, Jr.; the latter afterwards became a union organiser and member of the Industrial Workers of the World. Mainwaring returned to London in the late 1890s, where he continued to advocate anarcho-syndicalism and joined protests against the Boer War. In a May 1934 article in *Freedom*, Mat Kavanagh recalled Mainwaring's dramatic gifts as a speaker, noting that 'It was a common thing for him to speak for four or five hours at a stretch, often during that time attracting two or three fresh crowds of people.' He died suddenly while addressing a meeting at Parliament Hill Fields in 1907. His 'Reminiscences of William Morris, By a Working Colleague' appeared in the December 1896 *Freedom*. The 11 November 1911 issue of *Freedom* commem-orating its twenty-fifth anniversary records a speech in which Tarrida del Marmol praises the work of 'good old Sam Mainwaring, to whose energy we owed the few numbers of the paper *The General Strike*, and who... lived and died in the movement'. A brief life and photograph of Sam Mainwaring appears at libcom.org.

MASON, Stephen, 1832–1890

Author of pamphlets on commercial and financial subjects, Glasgow merchant and past president of the Glasgow Chamber of Commerce, from 1881–88 Stephen Mason was a Gladstonian Liberal MP for Lanarkshire, Mid-Division and supporter of Irish Home Rule..

MORDHURST, CLAUS HENRY, 1840–96

Born in Prussia, Mordhurst was active in the Prussian social democratic movement before moving to London in the late 1860s–early 1870s. The 1871 census recorded him as a piano maker living in the St. Pancras area of London, and by the mid-1870s he was living in Hammersmith with his wife and children. When he was proposed for membership at the fourth meeting of the Hammersmith Branch of the Democratic Federation, Mordhurst listed his address as 8 Furber Street, Dalling Road, Hammersmith. He was a steady attender, active outdoor speaker, and contributor of many practical services to the Branch — he helped make a partition for the newsroom, made a box for contributions, and often served on arrangements subcommittees. Bernard Shaw mentions Mordhurst in his diary 1886–88 in association with his visits to Kelmscott House, as dining with Morris, Tarleton and others after meetings, and on one occasion walking with Shaw to Shepherds Bush Station (4 November 1888, *Bernard Shaw: The Diaries, 1885–89*, vol. 1, p. 429). In an 1888 letter to Bruce Glasier Morris describes him as 'a Holsteiner, a very staunch & good Fellow' (10 May, Kelvin 2:779). Mordhurst strongly supported the split with the SDF, adducing Lassalle as a precedent for local autonomy.

> Mr Mordhurst spoke of the starting of Socialism by Lasalle [sic] in Germany and of his aim to make the branches as self-supporting as possible. He compared the present split with the disruption of the Socialist party in Germany... he believed that disruption under such circumstances was necessary to education.
> (18 January 1885, Hammersmith Socialist Society Minutes)

Mordhurst was an occasional speaker for the SL and later the Hammersmith Socialist Society; e.g., the May 1893 *Hammersmith Socialist Record* listed his 5 May talk on the 'Hull [Dockers] Strike'. In 1890 he was also a member of the Hammersmith branch of the anarchist-leaning Federation of all Trades and Industries, which met at Kelmscott House in August 1890; the 30 August *West London Observer* reported Mordhurst's characterization of the Federation's executive as 'an absolutely incapable body led by the nose by schemers.' (p. 6) After his death in Hammersmith on 21 August 1896, the anarchist *Liberty* reported that socialists 'from all sections' were present at his funeral, with wreaths sent by the Hammersmith Liberal and Radical Club, Mrs. Mann of the Freethought Party and the Hammersmith Socialist Society. Mordhurst appears in the 1888 group photograph of the Socialist League in the far right of the back row.

MORRIS, JANE ALICE ('Jenny'), 1861–1935

William and Jane Morris's eldest daughter was a bright, serious child considered more intellectual than May, and keenly interested in her father's

Jane Morris 1879 (Courtesy of the National Portrait Gallery)

political activities. In 1878 she began to suffer from a mysterious disease which resulted in violent seizures, and eventually in progressive physical and mental degeneration. Morris believed her condition was hereditary and blamed himself. Amidst his endless activities, he wrote her many long, affectionate, and politically detailed letters, among the best he wrote. After William's death, Jane Morris cared for her daughter for several years with the help of a nurse, and when this became too difficult Jenny was placed under private care. A few of Jenny's letters are preserved in the British Library and the Victoria and Albert Museum. Surviving documents are reticent about her condition; it has been sometimes diagnosed as 'epilepsy', but it is difficult to be certain what it was. See also footnotes [39] and [50].

MORRIS, JANE BURDEN, 1840–1914

The second child of Ann Maizey Burden and Robert Burden, an Oxford stableman, Jane Burden married Morris in 1859 at the age of nineteen, and with him raised two children: Jane Alice ('Jenny'), born 1861, and May, born 1862. Jane was considered an expert needlewoman, and early in their marriage the Morrises shared an interest in developing techniques of embroidery and weaving. Later Jane supervised some of the weavers employed by Morris and Co.. and embroidered for special clients of the Firm until Morris's death. After the birth of her children Jane suffered from problems of the back and spine which she attempted to cure with foreign trips, including travels to Italy with the Howard family. In addition to managing the Morris household and training her daughters, after Jenny developed mysterious seizures in 1878 Jane helped care for her daughter until her own death. Jane's lengthy friendship and briefer affair with the painter and poet Dante Gabriel Rossetti grieved Morris, but he showed a tolerance remarkable for the period in quietly accepting his wife's freedom of choice, and his later socialist writings advocate economic independence and sexual freedom for women. Jane's letters reveal her as a somewhat invalided but kindly and intelligent woman with literary and artistic interests, and she maintained warm friendships with Crom Price and other members of the Morris circle. Though lukewarm toward Morris's socialist activities, she took an interest in contemporary affairs; after Morris's death she and May joined the Fabian Society. Morris's letters indicate that despite disappointments, he continued to feel genuine affection for her. After his death Jane lived quietly at Kelmscott Manor with Jenny until the latter's condition required additional care. In the introductions to her father's *Collected Works*, May Morris seldom mentions her mother, but Jane's later letters seem to indicate a harmonious relationship with her daughter. For further discussion, see Frank Sharp and Jan Marsh, eds., *The Collected Letters of Jane Morris*, 2012.

MOWBRAY, CHARLES WILFRED, 1856–1910

Born in Bishop Auckland, Durham, after a stint in the army Charles Mowbray moved to Whitechapel in the East End of London, where he worked as a tailor and became an activist anti-parliamentarian and printer of left-wing literature. He began as a co-worker with Frank Kitz in the Labour Emancipation League before joining the SL upon its formation in 1885. A member of the League's anarchist wing and an active worker in the effort to establish the right to open-air speech, Mowbray was arrested in 1885 along with several others after a socialist meeting at Dod Street, Stepney, in East London, and again in 1886 in

Stratford, and as the *Diary* records, at Norwich in 1887, where he was sentenced to nine months hard labour. Morris's reservations about Mowbray's conduct are indicated in a letter to Joseph Lane:

> ... I see clearly that the Norwich Branch cannot keep Mowbray; so to London he had better come... As to any harm he may do, we must make the best of it. I believe him to be sincere; and we all know the faults of his character, and so I hope can guard against them. (4 February 1889, Kelvin 3:27, BL Add. MS 45,345)

Later Mowbray worked in the dockers' and tailors' strikes of 1889–90, and during the early 1890s was an active propagandist for anarchism, forming close ties with East End Jewish tailors and speaking at the Berners Street anarchist club. In 1891 along with Henry Charles and others Mowbray conducted anti-militarist propaganda at army barracks in Rochester, Colchester, and Chatham, and joined a No-Rent agitation in the Boundary Street East End slum where he lived. In 1892 he joined Louise Michel in a fundraising event on behalf of the Yiddish-language anarchist paper *Arbeter Fraynd*.

After Morris relinquished control of *Commonweal* in 1890, Mowbray continued as its publisher and wrote its first article in open advocacy of the use of dynamite. When in April 1892, in the Walsall anarchist case, a judge sentenced three anarchists framed by police agents to prison terms of ten years, and a fourth to five years, *Commonweal* editor David Nicoll wrote an article advocating political murder, for which he and Mowbray were arrested. Mowbray's wife Mary, the daughter of a former Communard Joseph Benoit, had died a day or two before of consumption at the age of thirty-eight, and his arrest meant the abandonment of five children (Charles, John, Richard, Grace, and Frederick). Morris paid Mowbray's bond of £500, and the case was later dismissed. Mary Mowbray's funeral was attended by a procession of several thousand people in recognition of her anarchist ties.

According to Paul Avrich's *An American Anarchist* (Princeton 1978, p. 102 ff.), Mowbray emigrated to the US in 1894, where he lectured in several cities. His obituary in the *Shoreditch Observer* in December 1910 described him as 'a sinewy, athletic black-haired determined man with the... tempestuous eloquence that stirred many an open-air meeting,' but Emma Goldman noted her opinion that his speeches lacked content. (Harry Kelly, *Roll Back the Years*, p. 102, cited in Avrich, p. 104) With associates, he founded *The Rebel* in Boston in 1894, was deported to Britain in 1900, and appeared in the 1901 census as living with his second wife Charlotte Smith and their children at 31 Eve Road, Plaistow, East London. He continued speaking for anarchism in London for a time; in 1905 he chaired a Whitechapel strike meeting attended by 5000 persons, with many turned away. He later became a tariff reform lecturer, and died in Bridlington, Yorkshire in 1910. See also footnote [3] and Nick Heath, 'Charles Mowbray,' at libcom.org. Details of Mowbray's later political activities may also be found at http://www.e7-nowandthen.org/2017/09/charles-mowbray-anarchist-revolutionary.html

REUSS, KARL THEODOR, 1855–1923

Later revealed as a spy in the pay of the Berlin political police, Reuss was a journalist and London correspondent for several foreign newspapers, who joined the SL in February 1885 and was elected to the Executive Committee. As a result of accusations by Victor Dave, who believed the police had acted on the basis of information only Reuss could have given them, Reuss was expelled from the SL on 10 May 1886, and Dave published an article exposing him in the 3 July 1886 *Freiheit*. Joseph Peukert, the leader of the *Gruppe Autonomie*, distrusted Dave, and so took Reuss with him to Belgium over New Year 1887, where Reuss was able to identify to the police the important anarchist John Neve. Neve was arrested on 21 February 1887, and on 13 May 1887 the *Socialdemokrat* printed an article on Neve's arrest which could only have been written by someone involved in the affair, and a meeting of anarchists and socialists later in May appointed a commission to investigate charges of Peukert's complicity with the police. Although the commission cleared Peukert, Peukert and Dave continued to attack each other in print and accuse each other of aiding the police, until Reuss himself wrote a long article for the 5 October *London Evening News* exposing the activities of London anarchist clubs, and Peukert wrote an article in *Die Autonomie* which attacked Reuss as a traitor. In this sordid and tragic episode, Peukert's political life was destroyed, Dave was discredited, and Neve's imprisonment and subsequent death in prison deprived European anarchism of one of its most important members. Reuss returned to Germany, and spent much of his later life as an officer of the Freemasons. (Andrew Carlson, *Anarchism in Germany*, Chap. 11) See also footnotes [56]–[58].

SCHEU, ANDREAS, 1844–1927

Scheu was a Viennese furniture designer who had been converted to socialism through listening to German followers of Ferdinand Lassalle. He became a confederate of Johann Most and an active figure in German anarchist politics, one of the founding members of the German Social Democratic Party, and editor of the socialist *People's Will*. Tried for treason by the Austrian government in 1870, he was sentenced to five years in prison, amnestied, and again tried and imprisoned briefly before leaving for London in 1874. There he joined the German leftist Rose Street Club, but became disaffected with German emigré factionalism, and joined the DF and SDF. One of the events which precipitated the 1885 SDF/SL split was Hyndman's denunciation of Scheu, and Scheu left to form the SL with Morris; Thompson notes that his dislike of Hyndman's chauvinism caused him to urge Morris to assume leadership. (p. 343) Scheu worked closely with Morris until his move to Edinburgh in 1885, where he became a salesman for Jaeger. Morris trusted him, wrote him some of his fullest and most reflective letters, and in an 1885 letter to May speaks of his 'tremendous energy and his knowledge of organisation'. (14 April, Kelvin 2:420, BL Add. MS 45,341) Articles by

Andreas Scheu (Courtesy of the Shaw Collection,
London School of Economics)

Scheu entitled 'Sincerity and Devotion' and a three-part 'What's to be Done?' appeared in the April, May, June and September 1885 *Commonweals*. That Scheu was considered an effective speaker is indicated by the Council's choice of him to debate with Bradlaugh; he was also a good singer and, like Morris, wrote Socialist songs (see his 'Song of Labour' with two settings, in *Chants of Labour*, ed. Edward Carpenter, London 1888, pp. 60-63). Although he was less active in the '90s, the *Labour Annual* of 1900 lists him in their 'Directory of Social Reformers', giving his address as 78, St John's Park, Blackheath, London, SE. After receiving a pension in 1911, he returned to Germany, and in 1923 published his reminiscences, *Umsturzkeime: Erlebnisse Eines Kaempfers* (Vienna), which emphasise his early revolutionary activities, but include a strongly laudatory chapter on Morris, Morris's letters to Scheu in German translation, and several of his songs. He seems someone who would have been more influential had he not had to divide his efforts between two countries and languages; his relationship with Morris merits further study. His English and German correspondence, preserved in the IISH in Amsterdam, documents his close ties with leading continental socialists as well as with the Morris family.

SHAW, GEORGE BERNARD, 1856–1950

The prominent playwright, critic, and Fabian was born in Dublin, to an Irish father of genteel pretensions and uncertain occupation, and a mother who left his father for London when G.B. Shaw was sixteen in an attempt to support herself and Shaw's two sisters by teaching music. After a few years as an estate agent's clerk, Shaw moved to London in 1876, and under financial constraints produced five novels between 1878 and 1883, served as art critic for the *World*, 1886–89, and music critic for the *Star*, 1888–90, and in 1892 began a career as a playwright with mild anti-establishmentarian tendencies. After an initial study of Henry George and Marx in French translation, in 1884 Shaw became a Fabian, but maintained friendly associations with the SDF and SL. Morris had admired Shaw's early novels, often invited him to speak at the Hammersmith Branch SL, and enjoyed his company, but by 1887 they were drifting apart. The *Diary* indicates Morris's exasperation at Shaw's tolerance of Bradlaugh's individualism; in June 1887 he described Shaw to Glasse as tending 'towards individualist anarchism' (17 June, Kelvin 2:670), and the two differed strongly over the desirability of parliamentary gradualism; Shaw's two articles in *Fabian Essays on Socialism* which he (Shaw) edited in 1889, 'The

May Morris, George Bernard Shaw, H.H. Sparling and Emery Walker 1889
(Courtesy of The Wilson: The Cheltenham Art Gallery and Museum)

Transition to Social Democracy' and 'The Impossibility of Anarchism', are in part attempted rebuttals of positions Morris had taken; Morris in turn reviewed them for *Commonweal* on 25 January 1890. Yet in 1893 Shaw co-operated with Morris in an attempt to formulate a platform for socialist union, and in 1895 published a defence of Morris and other Victorian artists against Max Nordau's charges of immorality in *Degeneration*.

Most important, Shaw's 1936 *William Morris As I Knew Him* is perhaps the best known memoir of Morris, and influenced interpretations of the latter's work for at least two decades. In many respects it is a moving tribute to Morris's character and expertly captures nuances of his temperament, but its method of contrasting Morris's character with Shaw's own becomes inevitably double-edged, a defence of Shaw's Fabianism and more 'rationally' sceptical modes of analysis. The claim that Morris is 'our one acknowledged great man' is less convincing in the absence of respect for Morris's actual personal, literary, and political choices; e.g, Morris's poetry is praised as lighthearted and facile, if sometimes sentimental, and though Shaw admires *Sigurd* and the socialist essays, he gives no clear idea of their impressive features.

Most pointedly, though, he finds Morris's political associates repellent:

> Unfortunately they had no experience of the government of anything more complicated than a coster's barrow; and they were romantic anarchists to a man, strong on the negative side, but regarding the State as an enemy, very much as the child regards the policeman... A very amateurish plan, called Anti-State Communism, was evolved; and its authors, after spending a good deal of Morris's money, suddenly perceived that the logic of their plan involved the repudiation of Morris's directorship, which was keeping the whole affair together. So Morris, who had been holding the League up by the scruff of its neck, opened his hand, whereupon it dropped like a stone into the sea, leaving only a little wreckage to come to the surface occasionally and demand bail at the police court or a small loan. (*AWS*, 2:xvi)

If there is enough truth to these charges so that they sting, enough contempt resides in the metaphor of the anarchist SL as a composite stray dog to be drowned or its more beleagured members as 'a little wreckage' to establish Shaw's real antipathy to Morris's basic egalitarian ideals. Morris was capable of rage and contempt for the strong but not the weak, and not only children are properly wary of police and the massed power of a state in which they have no means of representation. Had Morris's comrades been totally bereft of ideology, 'organisation', and character, the status of 'prophet and saint' Shaw is so willing to accord Morris would have been strangely hollow, and Morris's 'prophetic' gift one of inconsistency and bad judgement. Shaw's essay concludes with a climactic assertion which has often been quoted:

> And with such wisdom as my years have left me I note that as he has drawn further and further away from the hurly burly of our personal contacts into the impersonal perspective of history he towers greater and greater above the horizon beneath which his best advertised contemporaries have disappeared. (xl)

Would Morris have wanted such a subtly apolitical canonisation? The tribute is in good part a comment on Shaw, perhaps, and an act of nostalgic love for a long-dead spiritual parent. But a more measured and concrete respect for the intelligence and consistency of Morris's ideas and acts would serve his memory at least as well as such apotheosis as a heroically misguided eccentric. A good treatment of the Shavian-Morris relationship appears in chap. V of John Hulse, *Revolutionists in*

London (London 1970), to which I am indebted. See also footnotes [52] and [60].

SPARLING, HENRY HALLIDAY, 1860–1924

May Morris left behind few records of the man from whom she separated several years after their marriage, and Morris's contemporary biographer, J. W. Mackail, discreetly avoids mentioning him; someone has scratched 'Mrs Sparling' out of the Kelmscott Manor Guest Book and replaced it with 'May Morris'. The *Labour Annual* for 1895 lists Sparling as educated at Clifden, Connemara, 'by historical studies drawn towards Socialism', and an advocate of total abstinence. Sparling was a steady worker at Socialist League propaganda from 1885 to 1891, serving as League Council member 1885–88, secretary July 1885-December 1886, and subeditor under Morris of *Commonweal*, December 1886–May 1891. He was one of the SL speakers arrested on 8 February 1886 for alleged incendiary remarks ('bread or lead') at a Hyde Park demonstration. *Commonweal* indicates that he was a frequent speaker at meetings; as sub-editor he wrote numerous if rather wooden notes on current events, and his letters and comments indicate sympathy with Morris's role in League affairs. Although Thompson describes him as 'an unreliable ally' (Thompson, p. 523), he seems to have voted as an anti-parliamentarian.

Both William and Jane were unenthusiastic about the marriage, perhaps in part on prudential grounds. Scheu's letters to Sparling in the IIHS express amused sympathy with the latter over Morris's reported disapproval of the match, assuring Sparling that Morris will surely come round, and Jane's letters to Rosalind Howard reveal at least some skepticism: 'May's love affair has not progressed since you saw the lovers, they are... no nearer marrying as far as one can see. May rightly insists on employment being found by her fiancé before she marries and I strongly uphold her.' (31 June 1887, Sharp and Marsh, *Letters of JM*, p. 153) Morris tried to help on the employment front; on June 7th, 1887 he wrote to Liberal M.P. James Bryce: 'A friend of mine is a candidate for the librarianship of the National Liberal Club. His name is H.H. Sparling: he has some literary attainments, and a really good knowledge of books, and is an enthusiastic person about them. He is a man of high principle and very industrious and painstaking, and (if that be a qualification for a librarian's post) remarkably good-tempered.' (Kelvin 2:666) Even allowing for the context, Morris must have felt some goodwill toward his future son-in-law. The couple married in summer 1890, and in the end Morris employed Sparling at the Kelmscott Press 1890–94.

As late as April 1892 Sparling was listed in *Freedom* as lecturing for the Hammersmith Socialist Society, but he became a Fabian in the same year, and as Fabian delegate to a socialist Unemployed Organisation Committee argued against 'irresponsible' relief to the unemployed. The 1895 *Labour Annual* described him as 'now chiefly occupied with historical development of the Socialist movement' (p. 187), and in the 1897 *Labour Annual* he was still listed in the directory of 'Social Reform Lecturers'.

G.B. Shaw claimed that after a period in which he lived with the Sparlings for several months at Hammersmith Terrace, May lost interest in her husband, Sparling left for France to seek work as a journalist, and May obtained a divorce; Shaw believed Sparling had remarried. (*Morris As I Knew Him*, p. 33) In 1887 Sparling edited an edition of Defoe's *Captain Singleton* and a collection of Irish poems and songs, and in 1888 he wrote a pamphlet on unemployment, *Men Versus Machinery*. In the 1890s he wrote introductions or edited several volumes for the Kelmscott Press and in 1912 he published a lecture on 'Needs and Ideals: being a lecture on the Science of Organisation delivered to the Organisation Society'. In 1914 he contributed an essay to the thirtieth year commemorative issue of *Justice*, in which he used the phrase 'we socialists', and advocated more study of applications of science at SDF branch meetings, so despite interest in Fabianism he seems to have joined the SDF. In 1924 Sparling published an adulatory memoir, *The Kelmscott Press and William Morris, Master Craftsman*, describing himself as Morris's 'adoring and eager disciple'; the intensity of his praise suggests that the years with Morris may have been the best of his life, and if much of its commentary is derivative, Sparling's own personal memories are lively and interesting. A postscript by Robert Steele remarks that Sparling had died directly after the book was finished, and comments on 'the considerable importance and bulk of his [Sparling's] writings' and 'the personal qualities which endeared him to a wide circle of friends'. H. Lee (*Social Democracy in Britain*, 1935, p. 82) states that Sparling emigrated to the US and died in Pasadena, California.

TARLETON, HENRY BLACKHURST, 1845–1910

Born in Walton, Liverpool, Tarleton was the son of a watch and clock maker and followed his father into this occupation. In 1868 he married

Mary Sarah Christian, and after her death in 1879 Tarleton moved to London, leaving his two children in Liverpool in the care of his mother-in-law. In 1885 he was living in one room at 17 Chancellors Road, Hammersmith, paying 6s. weekly rent. An anti-parliamentarian SL member, Tarleton joined the Hammersmith branch in March 1886, listing his address as 101 The Grove, Hammersmith (now in W5, Ealing Green). He was a frequent outdoor speaker and lecturer at Kelmscott House for the Hammersmith branch of the SL and later the Hammersmith Socialist Society (e. g., on 22 October 1887 he was an outdoor speaker at Fulham along with Morris, and on 13 March 1892 he lectured to the HSS at Kelmscott House on 'Socialism and Social Reform' (*Hammersmith Socialist Society Record*, March 1894, 4). Tarleton also played the character of 'Constable Potlegoff' in the League's October 1887 production of Morris's socialist comedy, *The Tables Turned; or, Nupkins Awakened*. He is frequently mentioned in Shaw's diaries for 1886–88 as present at dinner at Kelmscott House along with SL members Walker, Tochatti, Mordhurst, and others, and was remembered by Shaw as present at 'Bloody Sunday' in November 1887: 'Tarleton found me paralysed with terror and brought me on to the Square, the police kindly letting me through in consideration of my genteel appearance.' (Thompson, p. 500, Shaw, *Collected Letters*, vol. 1, p. 177) Tarleton served as a member of the League Council in 1887–88 and as the League's financial secretary in 1888, and became a delegate to the 1889 French International Working-Men's Congress, where he visited the cathedral at Rouen with Frank Kitz and Morris. In 1891 he drafted the first issue of the *Hammersmith Socialist Society Record*. Tarleton later became a Fabian.

In 1890 he was living at 135 The Grove, Hammersmith as a boarder paying 5s a week; the 1891 census describes him as a mathematical instrument maker and widower, forty-six years of age. In December 1894 he ran as a socialist candidate for the Hammersmith Vestry, polling 250 votes; Morris's 14 December letter to Georgiana Burne-Jones notes that he is going to vote for 'the twelve' [Guardians] on the day following; May Morris was also a candidate (Kelvin 4:243, n. 5), polling 414 votes. The 1901 census records 'Henry Tarleton', a fifty-six-year-old widower, born in Liverpool, and with the occupation of 'School Musical Instructor', now a pauper in the Fulham District Workhouse. He died in the Workhouse Infirmary, Saffron Waldon, Essex, October 1910, described on his death certificate as a 'journeyman of Hammersmith' and 'Electrical instrument maker'. Tarleton appears in the 1888 Socialist League group photograph in the back row, third from left. [source: Stephen Williams]

TOCHATTI, JAMES, 1853–1928

A merchant tailor, lecturer on reformist and quasi-scientific topics, and lifelong campaigner for communist anarchism, James Tochatti was born in Ballater, Aberdeenshire, the son of a police constable, Joseph Tochatti, and his wife Jane Cormack. By the mid-1860s his family were living in Leeds, where his mother was a teacher in the Railway Street Ragged School. James worked briefly as a stationer (1871 census) before becoming a tailor, and moved to Shoreditch, London sometime in the mid-1870s. There he became active in the National Secular Society and also developed an interest in phrenology and physiognomy; his lecture on 'Our faces, and how we come by them' was given at the Freethought Institute, Walworth in September 1877 and on several later occasions. (*South London Chronicle* 14 September 1877, p. 3) Still in East London at the time of the 1881 census, Tochatti described his occupation as 'memory lecturer and phrenologist'. In 1882 he moved to Hammersmith, where his campaigning to reduce the working hours of shop assistants resulted in arrest on a charge of riotous conduct. (*Illustrated Police News*, 7 October, p. 3) He was active in the Hammersmith Radical Club, where he met members of the Hammersmith SDF, and in January 1885 became a founding member of the Hammersmith branch of the Socialist League.

Tochatti was a frequent outdoor speaker for the branch, served as branch delegate to the 1886 League Conference, and contributed news, notes and articles to *Commonweal*. In November 1888, along with Morris, Cunningham-Graham, David Nicholl, and Sparling, he spoke at a joint SDF/SL meeting in Hyde Park held to commemorate the murdered Chicago martyrs and protest against the closure of Trafalgar Square to demonstrations. (*Lloyds Weekly News*, 18 November, 1888, p. 8) In 1889 he helped organise a strike at Thornycroft's engineering factory, and in the early 1890s he served as organizing secretary of the United Shop Assistants' Union and was twice arrested on charges of creating 'disturbance' during protest demonstrations. (*West London Observer*, 6 September, 1890, p. 3; *Morning Post*, 17 October 1991, p. 2) *The Times* reported his remarks to an audience of about 1000 at an anarchist meeting held in conjunction with an 1892 Hyde Park May Day demonstration in support of an eight-hour day:

When they saw that the average wage of a working man in this country was 18 shillings per week, and that the average age of the working man 29 years, while the masters live in luxury to the age of 55, surely it was time to fight for their just rights. (Cheers). The eight hours demonstration was a farce. With the machinery of the present age the masters could get as much work out of a man in eight hours as seven years ago he [sic] got in twelve. He maintained that the workers could obtain an eight hour day at once if they resorted to the simple method of stopping at that time. (Hear, hear). It was no use cringing and asking Parliament to grant this or that boon; the workers had the power in their own hands, and they were fools if they did not use it. (2 May 1892, p. 7)

By the 1891 census Tochatti was listed as a merchant tailor in Hammersmith, with a shop on Beadon Road, W, described in *Liberty* as 'Carmagnole House.' As one of the SL's anarchist members Tochatti remained in the League after Morris's departure. *Freedom* of the early 1890s indicates that he spoke frequently, and the *Scotsman* reported that he had been physically attacked by thugs when speaking on behalf of anarchism at the 1894 annual May 1st labour demonstration (2 May, p. 7); in the same year he spoke to the Aberdeen Anarchist Communist Group on 14 October on 'Human Nature and Anarchism' and on 15 October on 'Economic Conditions and Anarchism'. (*Aberdeen Evening Express*, 13 October, 1894, p. 3) In 1896 he served as secretary of a group protesting against the exclusion of anarchists and 'non-political' delegates from the London International Socialist Workers and Trades Union Congress.

Commonweal reported that at a meeting held in November 1892 at the South Place Institute to commemorate the deaths of the Chicago anarchists, Tochatti had urged verbal restraint:

Tochatti objected to the wild language. We must not indulge in wild talk about dynamite and pillage (cries of dissent). As for dynamite, he was as ready to use it as any man, when the time came but any talk of its present use was madness. (Oh!) If we want to learn how to preach anarchy let us study the speeches of our Chicago comrades, and learn to explain our noble principles in the same clear and plain fashion. (*Commonweal*, 21 November 1891, p. 150)

Tochatti's enthusiastic defence of the imprisoned anarchist David Nicoll is recorded in the December 1892 *Freedom*, p. 1. Despite his strong support of Nicoll he must have had reservations about some of the public statements of his fellow anarchists, for in January 1894, disturbed by the incendiary tone of *Commonweal*, he began *Liberty*, considered by Quail an unusually open-minded anarchist journal. (p. 204) When in late 1893 Tochatti asked Morris for a contribution, Morris replied suggesting that Tochatti repudiate propaganda by violence, and added:

> However, I don't for a moment suppose that you agree with such 'propaganda by deed'. But since I don't think so, that is the very reason why I think you should openly say that you don't.
> (12 December 1893, Kelvin 4:113, WMorris Gal, J357)

Tochatti did provide this repudiation, and Morris contributed two essays to *Liberty*, 'Why I Am a Communist' (February 1894) and 'As to Bribing Excellence' (May 1895).

Tochatti published his 'Reminiscence of William Morris,' in the December 1896 issue of *Liberty* (p. 123), arguing that 'It is a great mistake to suppose that Morris changed his views with regard to parliamentary action. In a comparatively recent lecture at Kelmscott House he expressed his belief that the people were going that way, but he added with emphasis, 'Don't make the mistake of thinking this, Socialism.'' He noted that 'Like his friend Walter Crane, he helped all, being too great a man to be sectarian,' and promised more reminiscences and an account of Morris's letters to him on the topic of Socialism. This was the final issue of *Liberty*, however, and these reminiscences did not appear. Some years later Tochatti offered his memories of Morris at a gathering to commemorate Morris's death held at the William Morris Hall, 32 Upper Mall, Hammersmith, at which Walter Crane and Herbert Burrows also spoke, and Cunninghame-Graham sent a letter to be read. (*West London Observer*, 11 October 1907, p. 6)

Despite *Liberty*'s closure in 1896, however, Quail (pp. 273-74) states that in the early 1900s Tochatti was again a frequent speaker, and his tailoring store in Hammersmith became a meeting place for anarchist discussion. In 1909 his premises were searched by the police as part of an attempt to find incriminating evidence against Guy Aldred, who had recently been imprisoned for a year for publishing the anti-imperialist newspaper *Indian Sociologist*; Tochatti complained of 'a detective outrage more suited to Russia than England,' and London Labour MP Will Thorne raised the issue of possible police misconduct on his behalf in the House of Commons. (*The Scotsman*, 29 September 1909, p. 10)

The December 1912 *Freedom* announced Tochatti's 'Lantern Lecture' on 'Agriculture' at the Morris Studio, Adie Road, Hammersmith; in 1913 he urged an audience of omnibus workers who had waged a successful strike, 'irrespective of victory which they had won, to press forward and obtain fresh concessions. They were, he said, in a class war' (*West London Observer*, 26 September, 1913, p. 13); and on 12 October 1914, he was reported as lecturing in Bristol on 'The Attitude of Revolutionists towards the War' (*Freedom*, November 1914). John Mahon's *Harry Pollitt*, London 1976, pp. 65-66, describes Pollitt's visits to his shop in 1918 and after, where according to Pollitt he had

> defended conscientious objectors on socialist grounds,
> disputing with Tochatti, who alternatively favoured folded arms
> and shooting the officers. Sometimes they had first-hand news
> from Russia by someone returning from there.

In 1877 Tochatti married Louisa Susan Kaufman, of German descent, who had a fine singing voice used to perform at benefit events as 'the socialist songstress'. (*West London Observer*, 5 October 1889, p. 6) *Commonweal* reported in October 1889 that at a meeting in support of the Thornycroft strikers held on Acton Green and addressed by Tochatti and John E. Williams, 'Louisa Tochatti opened proceedings with the revolutionary song 'When the loafers are somewhere down below''. (5 October 1889, p. 318) [Composed by C. W. Beckett and published as 'Song for Socialism' in the 17 March 1888 *Commonweal*, this song continued to be used in labour movement circles into the early twentieth century.]

Louisa appears several times in the Hammersmith Socialist League minutes as present at meetings; on 10 February 1888 she reported to the branch that at a recent meeting in Parish Hall, Chelsea she had sold twenty-four *Commonweal*s, and she is mentioned in the 7 September 1889 *Commonweal* as collecting money for the London Dock strikers. According to libcom.org, she was also remembered as singing revolutionary songs at open-air meetings in the 1900s. By 1881 the couple had three children; among these was Moncure Douglas Conway Tochatti (Moncure Daniel Conway was a freethinker and minister at the South Place Chapel 1864–65 and 1893–97), who was born in Hammersmith in 1887. Moncure Tochatti (later Moncure Douglas Galdino) moved with his family to Bournemouth, and James Tochatti died in Poole, Dorset, near Bournemouth in 1928. I am indebted to

Stephen Williams for much of this information. For a fuller account of Tocchati's political career, see Stephen Williams and Florence Boos, *Useful and Beautiful* 2017.2 (available on the US William Morris Society website).

In the Hammersmith Socialist League group photograph Tochatti appears in the middle row, third from left. Louisa Tochatti is also listed by the National Portrait Gallery as present in a later, similar photograph though not identified.

VAN DER HOUT, ISAAC SALOMON, 1843–1918

Van der Hout was an Amsterdam tailor and anarcho-socialist who organized demonstrations in his home country and participated in the 1871 and 1872 Annual Conferences of the First International, during which he was a member of the anti-Marxist section. He moved to London in 1874 in search of work, and was active in East End left radical politics from the late '70s. He became a member of the Labour Emancipation League and later the Social Democratic Federation, joining the group which left to found the Socialist League in January 1885. Van der Hout was a member of the Hackney Branch and a frequent speaker; the 27 September 1884 *Justice* reported on a meeting of the Labour Emancipation League in Hoxton, East London: 'Mr Vanderhout addressed a good audience on 'Socialism v Bradlaughism' in the St. John's Hall, St. John's Road, on Sunday evening. The speaker's answers to the opposition were warmly applauded by the audience. Several joined the League at the close of the meeting.' He spoke along with Morris and German Socialist Friedrich Lessner at the 1885 Paris Commune Celebration, and the 30 July 1887 *Commonweal* noted that he was scheduled to speak at Beadon Road, Hammersmith on Sunday 31 July. Van der Hout was present at the massive free speech demonstration at Dod Street in 1885 and at demonstrations in support of the Dock Strike of 1889. After the dissolution of the Socialist League he reportedly joined the SDF and remained active in local working men's clubs in the East End. As late as 1896 *Reynolds Newspaper* reported his upcoming lecture at the Newington Reform Club, Clayton House, on 'Lords of the Land'. (5 April). A letter from him in the SL IISH archives gives a working-class Amsterdam address, 97 Waterlooplein; two 1886 letters to H. Halliday Sparling bear a return address of 19 Hanbury Street in Spitalfields. In 1891 the census listed him as living with his family in White's Row, Spitalfields with an occupation of 'rag sorter'; in 1911 he was still at

White's Row but listed as a 'Commission Agent.' He and his wife Sara Harpman (b. Amsterdam c. 1840) had three sons and a daughter. A brief biography of Van der Hout in Dutch appears on the BWSA site, a biographical dictionary of socialism and the labour movement, http://socialhistory.org/bwsa/biographie/hout. I am indebted for much of this information to Stephen Williams. See also footnote [150].

WALKER, EMERY, 1851–1933

An engraver and pioneer in typography and book design, Walker was born in Paddington, Middlesex, the son of coach builder Emery Walker and his wife Mary Anne. Forced to leave school at thirteen, he joined Alfred Dawson in conducting the Typographic Etching Company 1872–83, and in 1886 partnered with Walter Boutall to found a firm of engravers and art photographers, later Emery Walker, Ltd., with premises in Hammersmith. In 1877 he married Mary Grace Jones (1849/50–1920), with whom he had a daughter, Dorothy (1878–1963). In 1883 he met his Hammersmith neighbour William Morris, and together they undertook typographical experiments, on the basis of which Morris founded the Kelmscott Press in 1891, for which Walker served as advisor. Walker also joined Morris in working for the SPAB, the inauguration of the influential Arts and Crafts Exhibition Society in 1888, as a founding member of the Hammersmith Branch of the Socialist Democratic Federation in 1884, and later as a member of the Socialist League. He served as Branch secretary for several years, organizing the Sunday evening lectures. After Morris's death Walker founded the Doves Press in 1900 with T. Cobden-Sanderson, and co-managed it until 1909. His ideas for improved book design for ordinary as well as limited editions had a substantial effect on later British book production. The writer of his *ONDB* entry claims that 'his influence, direct or indirect, can be discerned in nearly every well-designed traditional typographical page that now appears.' (Sydney Cockerell, rev. John Trevitt, 2004). Walker's former house at 7 Hammersmith Terrace, decorated in Arts and Crafts style, is now preserved as a museum. In the 1888 Hammersmith Socialist League group photo, Walker is standing in the middle row to the left of Morris.

WARDLE, GEORGE Y., 1836–1910

A member of the Wardle family of dyers in Leek, he joined Morris and Co. as draughtsman and bookkeeper in 1866, and on Warrington

Taylor's death in 1870 became manager. In 1861 George Wardle married Madeleine ('Lena') Smith, who had been acquitted in Scotland after a trial for the murder of a former lover, and they had two children, Mary ('Kitten') and Thomas Edmund (born 1863 in Suffolk). George Wardle was also brother-in-law to Thomas Wardle, founder of the Wardle and Co. silkworks, with whom Morris co-operated from 1875 in the development of vegetable dyes. Both George and Thomas Wardle were members of the SPAB, and George Wardle had been designated as their emissary to investigate restorations at St Mark's in Venice. In 1880, three years before he joined the Democratic Federation, Morris asked Wardle to draw up a plan for employee profit-sharing within Morris and Co., which he then adopted. In 1886 Morris estimated that under this plan he had made £1,800, and as the Queen Square store manager George Wardle had made £1,200.

Morris biographers have on occasion confused George and Thomas Wardle, and to compound the difficulty confuse each of these in turn with George J. Wardle, a labour poet, editor of the *Railway Reviewer*, and member of the ILP, and Thomas E. Wardle, George Wardle's son, a cabinetmaker and active member of the Socialist League. By contrast, May Morris describes this George Wardle as 'a man who stood aloof from politics and watched all enthusiasms with equanimity' (introduction, *CW*, 16:xi), and a long 1898 letter from Wardle to Sidney Cockerell giving his memories of Morris's political activities (reprinted in *AWS*, 2:602-606) confirms this. Wardle states that he was unsympathetic to politics and 'was obliged to discourage Morris from talking politics all day, which he gladly would have done, at that time.' Nonetheless he shared some of Morris's aims, writing to Sydney Cockerell of Morris: 'The education of the workman of course always remained the end and motive of [his] political action, for he could not see more clearly as he endeavored to carry forward his artistic principles that it was hopeless to expect intellligent co-operation from workers who were not free to use their intelligence...' (605-6)

By contrast his wife, Lena Wardle, joined the Socialist League and at the time of the *Diary* was a member of its council. She organized fundraising efforts and in 1885 became treasurer of the newly established Bloomsbury branch, and as the caretaker of the 'Missionary Fund' supported the efforts of Donald and Mahon to run socialist electoral candidates. She also edited the brief-lived *Red Rag: An Un-Official Organ of International Democracy* (two issues, January 1891), detailing the activities of the United Democratic Club of 57/58 Chancery Lane, London, on whose management committee she served. Their daughter Mary married John Rigby, a member of the Bloomsbury Branch of the Socialist League, and their son Thomas Edmund Wardle (1863–1931?), as mentioned above, was an art cabinet-maker with a workshop at Sandland Street, Bedford Row. Thomas also joined the Bloomsbury branch, becoming its secretary 1885–86 and a member of the League Council for 1885 and 1886. In 1886 he was arrested four times for public speaking on behalf of the League at Stratford, Paddington, and Marylebone, and in 1892 he gave testimony at the trial of David Nicholl and Charles Mowbray. Though the identification is uncertain, he may be the Thomas E. Wardle whose death on 21 September 1931 was reported by the *New York Times*.

George Wardle worked daily with Morris for twenty-five years. Although he claimed that he 'never had the disposition for the part of Boswell', at the request of Morris's biographer J. W. Mackail he provided a neatly-written thirty-one-page commentary on the history of Morris and Co., with a brief appendix on the ethos of its workplace, noting that 'No-one having worked for Mr. Morris could willingly have joined another workshop or, having passed through any other, would have given up Mr. Morris's for that.' (B. L. Add. MS. 45,350; Charles Harvey and Jon Press, *Art, Enterprise and Ethics: The Life and Works of William Morris*, 1996, pp. 82-115)

After retiring from Morris and Co. in 1890, Wardle devoted himself to the study of medieval church ornamentation. May Morris comments on Wardle's 'beautiful drawings of the screens in Norfolk churches in the Victoria and Albert Museum', (*AWS*, 2:xvii), and between 1891 and 1896 he made frequent trips to Italy to examine its art and architecture. After his death his widow moved to the United States, remarried, and died in poverty in 1928 at the age of ninety-three. (Mary Hartman, *Victorian Murderesses*, New York 1977, p. 83) Wardle's notes on his Italian journeys and essays on the art of Pisa and Ravenna are deposited in the Victoria and Albert Museum, and a sympathetic account of both Wardles is provided by Yvonne Kapp, *In Search of Mr. and Mrs. Wardle*, History Workshop Pamphlet, 1994.

WARREN, CHARLES, 1840–1927

Warren was an archaeologist, police commissioner noted for severity, and British military commander. After publishing three books on his excavations in Jerusalem, and serving in several British imperialist campaigns (the Kaffir War, 1878; the Egyptian campaign of 1882; Arabia and Bechuanaland, 1884–85; and Suakim (in the Sudan), 1886), Warren was elected Commissioner of the London Metropolitan Police in 1886. He was responsible for the police suppression at Trafalgar Square in November 1887, which caused more than 100 casualties and two deaths among members of the crowd. Methods assumed abroad apparently seemed harsh at home, and complaints of his severity may have contributed to his resignation from office in 1888 in a dispute with the Home Secretary over police autonomy. In *News from Nowhere*, Morris's portrayal of a reactionary general is based on Warren. From 1889–1900 he served as a British military commander in China and South Africa, and after returning to England in 1900, he devoted his time to working with the Boy Scouts and writing on archaeological and religious subjects.

WATTS, JOHN HUNTER, 1853–1923

An active secularist in his native city of Manchester, J. Hunter Watts published *The Poets of Great Britain* in 1878 (reprinted from essays in the *Republican Chronicle*). He became an early and lifelong member of the SDF, was elected SDF treasurer when Morris's group seceded to form the Socialist League in 1885, and participated in the 8 February 1886 procession of the unemployed to Hyde Park. His friend H. Lee described him as an ardent campaigner for the SDF, but personally fond of Morris:

> Though a great admirer of William Morris, Watts remained with the SDF at the split of 1884, but his friendship for William Morris made him a little more kindly disposed towards the Socialist League than some of us liked!... No one could have been animated with greater missionary zeal for the socialist cause... I have known him to go out alone into some poverty stricken East End district of London, and with a flag and a box break new ground and hold a meeting in the open air if he could keep a dozen or so people around him. (*Social Democracy in Britain*, London 1935, pp. 85-86)

On a tour in the fall of 1888 Morris stayed with Watts in Manchester, describing him in a letter to his daughter Jenny as 'a very good fellow' (4 December, Kelvin 2:839). His article, 'Growing Respectable', appeared in the *Commonweal* of 30 March 1889. In 1895 Watts became a member of the newly organised executive council of the SDF, and in 1906 he strongly opposed a movement to affiliate with the ILP (Tsuzuki, *Hyndman and British Socialism*, p. 163). He remained with the organisation when in 1912 it became the British Socialist Party, and in 1916 he followed Hyndman into its pro-war offshoot, the National Socialist Party. Watts was an early advocate of Socialist Sunday Schools, and in 1904 wrote *State Maintenance for School Children*; in later life he spoke against toleration of syndicalists within the BSP (Tsuzuki, pp. 132-33). His account was one of several included in *Why I Became a Socialist*, a collection of reminiscences by early Socialist pioneers published by the Twentieth Century Press, n.d. In this he describes his first meeting with Morris after one of the latter's lectures at the South Place Chapel, 'I reminded him of some lines in the prologue to the Earthly Paradise: 'Dreamer of dreams born out of my due time,/ Why should I strive to set the crooked straight?'.... To my remark 'You seem to be striving to set the crooked straight,' he replied, 'I wrote that before I became a Socialist.' (32-33)

WATTS (later WATTS-DUNTON), (WALTER) THEODORE, 1832–1914

A solicitor, literary critic, minor author and friend of authors, Theodore Watts attended Cambridge and practised law for a period in London. There he became the legal counsellor and friend of the poet and painter D.G. Rossetti, and later of the poet A.C. Swinburne, whom he cared for in his Putney home from 1879 until Swinburne's death in 1909. As literary critic for the *Examiner* after 1874, and of the *Athenaeum* from 1876 to 1898, he encouraged many younger authors. In 1897 and 1898 he published a book of poems and a novel based in part on his pre-Raphaelite associates, *Aylwin*, and a second novel appeared posthumously. He added his mother's surname 'Dunton' in 1896. Watts-Dunton effusively but shallowly praised Morris in the two chapters devoted to him in his posthumous memoirs, *Old Familiar Faces* (1916).

WEBB, PHILIP SPEAKMAN, 1831–1915

A lifelong friend and co-worker of Morris, versatile and active designer for Morris and Co., and prominent Victorian architect, Webb was educated in a Northamptonshire Grammar School and trained in sketching and drawing. Upon the death of his father when he was seventeen, he abandoned earlier plans to become an artist and articled with a Berkshire architect before returning to Oxford in 1854 to work as an assistant to Gothic revivalist G.B. Street. He met Morris when the latter joined Street's firm as a pupil in January 1856, and when Street

Philip Webb (Courtesy of the National Portrait Gallery)

moved his office to London later in the year, he joined the circle of Morris's artistically-inclined Oxford friends who surrounded D.G. Rossetti. His first architectural commission was the building of Red House for Morris in 1859 (now owned by the National Trust), conceived as an experiment in vernacular simplicity of construction, and which would later serve as a model for arts and crafts designers. A founding member of the Firm in 1861, Webb drew animals, birds, and traceries and designed stained glass, embroidery, tiles, metal work, candlesticks, jewelry, furniture, wall decorations and tapestries. His memories of the Firm's early days stress its communal features:

> The best of those times was that there was no covetousness; all went into common stock — and then, we were such boys. (W.R. Lethaby, *Philip Webb and His Work*, Oxford 1935, p. 62)

Later as an independent architect Webb designed thirty-five complete houses and one church, including Clouds, Wiltshire (1881–86), Standen, Sussex (1892), and St. Martin's Church, Brampton, Cumberland (1877–78), supervising all the details of construction.

In the 1870s Webb designed a cover for Morris's *Sigurd the Volsung*. In 1876 he joined Morris in founding and working for the Society for the Protection of Ancient Buildings, developing a method for cleaning out loose core materials to strengthen decaying walls. Webb and Morris shared an early interest in Ruskin and the Gothic revival, and both respected the decorative art of other countries as well as the traditional British architecture of the Oxford and English countryside; they also loved arduous and detailed artwork in almost any media, as well as the natural qualities of building materials, and they shared a vigorous hatred of the commercial greed intensified by the Industrial Revolution. Like Morris, Webb joined the Social Democratic Federation in 1883 and in 1885 affiliated with the Bloomsbury branch of the Socialist League, serving as the League's treasurer. Webb never married; his letters in the Victoria and Albert Museum to William and Jane Morris reveal deep affection for both. His first biographer, W. R. Lethaby, barely mentions his socialism, but some of his comments on industrialism in 1901 suggest some of the views he shared with Morris:

> By the herding of labouring men like herrings in a barrel it had been found out that a class of rich people could be produced whose greed could grasp more than 'the dreams of avarice' had forecast. Well, is there any sign in this new-born century that the greed-god is about to be knocked off its pedestal? (Lethaby, p. 11)

Webb designed Morris's coped gravestone, saying, 'It will be a roof for the old man' (Lethaby, p. 130), and remarked of his death, 'My coat feels thinner... He is not dead after all... But one would think I had lost a buttress.' (Lethaby, p. 195) In 1900 Webb retired to a cottage in Sussex, but designed two cottages at Kelmscott Manor for his old friend Jane Morris, with whom he corresponded until her death. His first biographer, W. R. Lethaby, described him as a man of ready wit and simple tastes, who avoided public praise and aimed 'to consume the least possible, yet without impoverishment.' (Lethaby, p. 252) He is the subject of a 2005 biography, *Philip Webb: Pioneer of Arts and Crafts Architecture* by Sheila Kirk, who is also the author of his *ODNB* entry. See also footnote [88].

WILLIAMS, JOHN EDWARD ('Jack'), c. 1854–1917

Described by fellow SDF member Harry Quelch as 'short and sturdy, bent of back and strong of limb, with a strong voice, rugged, weather-

Jack Williams (*Social Democracy in Britain*, H.W. Lee, London, 1935)

beaten features, and dark bushy hair and beard' (*How I Became a Socialist*, Twentieth Century Press, n.d., p. 34), Williams was an unskilled labourer who had been raised in a succession of workhouses and had imbued Irish nationalist sympathies from an uncle and aunt. He joined the Rose Street Club and Irish Land League, helped Hyndman in establishing the DF and later the SDF, became a member of its first Executive Committee, and for almost thirty years was a constant organiser of meetings of the unemployed. In 1885 he was arrested at Dod Street and imprisoned for one month, and as an unsuccessful SDF candidate at Hampstead he polled only twenty-seven votes. He was arrested in a demonstration of the unemployed in February 1886, and again at Bell Street in April 1887; he joined in founding the National Federation of Labour (1886–94) along with John Ward, in 1889 aided in organizing a strike at a torpedo factory in Chiswick, and in the early 1890s helped lead mass protest meetings against unemployment on Tower Hill. In 1895 he was still a member of the reorganised SDF executive, and in 1906 as an SDF candidate for parliament in Northampton he polled 2,544 votes. In 1912 he retired on a small pension. His recollections are reprinted in *How I Became a Socialist*.

WILSON, CHARLOTTE MARTIN, 1854-1944

The daughter of Clementina and Robert Martin, a member of the Royal College of Surgeons, Charlotte attended Merton Hall (later Newnham College), Cambridge briefly in 1873-74, married her cousin Arthur Wilson, a London stockbroker, in 1876, and settled in Hampstead. Susan Hinely has noted a pattern of women-related and feminist concerns in Wilson's lifelong activism for philanthropic, progressive intellectual, and anarcho-socialist causes ('Charlotte Wilson, the 'Woman Question', and the Meanings of Anarchist Socialism in Late Victorian Radicalism,' *IRSH*, 2011). An officer of the London Society for the Extension of University Teaching in the late 1870s and the organizer of a North London branch of the Metropolitan Association for Befriending Young Servants in 1880, Wilson joined the Fabians in 1884 and founded a study society to read the works of continental socialists, among them Karl Marx and Pierre-Joseph Proudhon. She published a series of articles on anarchism, in *Justice* (1884), *The Anarchist* (1885), the *Practical Socialist*, and *Fabian Tracts* (1886); three of which were reprinted by Cienfuegos Press (1979, biographical introduction by Nicolas Walter). As revealed in these essays, Charlotte Wilson's 'anarchism' seems a rather abstract mixture of moral idealism, individualism, and collectivism:

> Anarchists believe that the solution of the social problem can only be wrought out from equal consideration of the whole of the experience at our command, individual as well as social, internal as well as external. (Walter, p. 1)

In several features her essays resemble those of Morris during the period: their holism about social revolution, attack on vaguely defined 'Monopoly', and emphasis on the satisfactions appropriate to work and art:

> When each person directs his own life, then, and then only, he throws his whole soul into the work he has chosen, and makes it the expression of his intensest purpose and desire, then, and then only, labour becomes a pleasure, and its produce a work of art. (Walter, p. 23)

What seems her one concrete suggestion for action, 'the direct seizure by the workers of the means of production' (Walter, p. 22), also resembles Morris's most frequently reiterated suggestion during this period, that of a general strike. Since they frequently spoke at the same meetings during this period, influence or cross-influence is conceivable, though Morris seems to have recorded no favourable responses.

Charlotte Martin (Wilson) at Newnham College, Cambridge
Charlotte is seated in the middle row, left
(Courtesy of The Principal and Fellows, Newnham College)

At a socialist conference in 1886 Wilson seconded an anti-parliamentary amendment by Morris, and in the same year she persuaded Kropotkin to join with her to found the journal *Freedom*, which she edited and largely subsidized until 1895. She also helped organize the annual commemorations of the Paris Commune and the 1886–87 effort to prevent the execution of the Chicago Haymarket anarchists. The *Daily News* reporter who attended the 1887 Paris Commune celebration described her speaking manner in rather gendered terms (18 March):

> Mrs. Wilson is a slender person, bordering on middle age, but on the right side of the border, dressed becomingly in black, and with hair trained forward in an ordered mass to form a sort of frame of jet for the thin, thoughtful face. The type is the South Kensington or British Museum art-student, the aesthete with 'views', and Mrs. Wilson quite realized it as to the views. She was decidedly Anarchical... What she did say was delivered with

great clearness of enunciation, with great purity of accent, with a certain appearance of effort, not to say of fatigue, as though the hall taxed her voice beyond its power, and with the monotonous calm that is perhaps the most common outward sign of the born fanatic. She was quite womanly and ladylike to use the good old-fashioned word. As she now and then refreshed her memory from her manuscript she exhibited a certain hesitation that had the effect at least of timidity, and that did not misbecome her sex and her evident good breeding. The great fault of the Commune, she said, was that it tried to form a Government, a regular orderly administration, with arbitrary powers; the great virtue of the Commune was that it brought men and women together into simpler social relations and truer brotherhood.

Charlotte Wilson left the Fabians in 1888, but later rejoined in order to work for women's suffrage, forming a Fabian Women's Group in 1908; after World War One she was the honorary secretary of a prisoner-of-war fund for a British regiment; and after her husband's death in 1932 she emigrated to the U.S.

A stockbroker's wife devoted to the abolition of arbitrary law and property distinctions, the only upper-middle class woman to propagate revolutionary anarchism in Britain during the 1880s, yet neither herself a labourer nor comfortable with working people, Charlotte Wilson's political views may seem to embody latent contradictions. Nonetheless in his 1891 *roman à clef*, *The Anarchists*, John Henry Mackay reproduces one of her passionate speeches on the Haymarket affair, noting that 'A few only in the meeting seemed to know her; but whoever knew her, knew also that she was the most faithful, the most diligent, and the most impassioned champion of Communism.' (pp. 41-43, cf. Nicholas Walter, 'Charlotte Wilson,' *ODNB*, 2004) Wilson also forms the model for 'Gemma' in Ethel Voynich's melodramatic 1897 novel of the Italian independence movement, *The Gadfly*. (Hinely, 24) See also footnotes [61] and [107].

Index